Breakup With A Smile!

Breakup With A Smile!

Laksh Kishore Malhotra

GenNext Publication

ISBN: 978-93-5324-106-3

Price : ₹ 360

First Published, 2017

Published by

GenNext Publication
5, Ansari Road
Daryaganj, New Delhi-110002
Phone: 9811692060
E-mail: gennextpublication@hotmail.com

Printed at: G. Print Process, Delhi.

Cataloging in Publication Data—DK
Courtesy: D.K. Agencies (P) Ltd. <docinfo@dkagencies.com>

Malhotra, Laksh Kishore, author.
Breakup with a smile! / Laksh Kishore Malhotra.
pages cm
Novel.
ISBN: 978-93-5324-106-3

1. Separation (Psychology)—Fiction. 2. Psychological fiction, Indic (English) 3. Romance fiction, Indic (English) I. Title.

PR9499.4.M35B74 2016 DDC 823.92 23

Dedicated to

My Parents

My Friends

Delhi Public School, Jammu

And

The Most Beautiful Smile on Earth!

Acknowledgements

Okay, so is this book getting published? Like really? You have picked it from a bookshelf or ordered online to read it? Why does it seem like a dream to me?

Before someone pinches me and breaks this happy dream of mine, let me thank those people without whom, this book would have been never possible.

There are a number of people I would like to thank.

Some for holding my hand and making me rise from bad times and some for putting me in bad times.

First, I would like to thank my family. My Mom, Meera and my Dad, Kishore; I love you both. Even though we fight sometimes, I love you both to infinity. I know I might sound a bit melodramatic, but you two are my God. Thank you for everything you have done till now.

My little sister Astha, for constantly peeking in my laptop's screen whenever I was typing something and asking me the same question every time, 'What is a break up?'

Second, my ninth standard's English teacher for making me feel as unwanted as Appendix. Here, the book you hold in your hand proves a point to her.

Third, my friends. Friends are something life would have been incomplete. I love you all. You are there to make this guy smile, hear his utter nonsense, motivate him all the time. Thank you!

My classmates: Aryan, Akshat, Priyanshu, Utkarsh (Sorry for…leave it!), Anirudh, Saksham, Mussharaf, all the girls, Sarah, Riga, Rupali, Farheen…

Special thanks to Riga for convincing me that if I tell my parents about my book, it won't bring apocalypse on earth.

My ex-classmates: Guntas, Dhruv, Ishan, Gurvind, Divyansh, Lakshit, Danish, Divyanshu, Pranav, Karanveer, Megha, Japneet, Gunjan, Etisha, Padam, Neharika, Aashita…so on. Though we are divided by streams, I still love you all. Sorry if I missed some names.

My Mains: Danish and Divyanshu. I love you both! We've been together since third standard. Damn these streams, I still love you even if I am the dumbest out of the three. Thanks for being my side.

My writer-dancer-painter friend Muskan Bakshi, for being the first reader of all of my works. Thanks for helping me through some of the parts of the book and believing in the fact that I could write. Motivation can never get any more beautiful!

My cross state Gujarati Friend, Jyotsna Miskeen. Thanks for pointing out the mistakes, giving me a chance to correct them and being so humble and highly motivating throughout the whole journey. I know my grammar sucks. I'll try my best to improve it. You are *Taylor Swift* times better than me!

My Bengali friend Mili. Thanks a lot! I can never thank you enough (You know why *Wink*)

Jaskirat, for making me smile like an idiot with those in-depth analysis of my book.

Big thanks to Mrs Poonam Chatoo, once my English teacher. You are the best mam! The best English teacher one could ever get. Thank you for being there mam!

All my English teachers, for supporting the writer in me.

My school, Delhi Public School, Jammu.

My extended family at Facebook, Instagram and Snap chat. The support you guys give sends thunderbolts down my spine.

My aunts and uncles from the maternal as well as paternal side.

My Grandparents.

The people at Gyan Books. Thank you all for your support and giving me a chance. Big thanks to the Director, Mr Amit Garg for being extremely helpful and answering to all my queries.

And Lastly,

My readers. As Michael Faudet once said, 'I write because you exist'.

You all are the real heroes behind this.

Well, had you guys not been there, this book would still have been sitting on a book shelf or displaying on an online shopping portal. Thank you for picking this book up. "Tu Jo Hai toh Main Hoon".

With this, I would like to welcome you to Breakup With A Smile!

PROLOGUE

I ordered the cheapest cold coffee for myself and sat down. I knew I had to eat something. *It has been three days now…Three days since she left me. Three days since I slept. Three days since I ate.*

I opened the front camera and saw my face in it. I looked weak. My eyes were swollen. *Break ups happen all the time! No need to act like an asshole!*

I sat on the table and sipped from my coffee. I looked at other people; mostly were couples. Don't know why but some of them were staring at me. Maybe it was my fucked up appearance.

I saw a group of girls sitting on the table next to me. To my horror they also stared at me. I gave them a wry smile and returned in my thoughts on how it was the second time my heart was broken. And I still couldn't do anything about it. *What do girls think huh? We can't live without them? They have the moral right to break hearts and screw boys?*

The girls started to laugh and talk about their boyfriends. I hated girls for every reason now. I wanted to shout at them to keep quiet and shut the fuck up but refrained myself.

'Why did you break up with him?' A girl in pink sweater said to the girl in black jacket, playing with her brownie. My ears alerted on the mention of a 'break up'.

'You know…he become serious…serious about the commitment' she said. I stopped for a few seconds and stared at her. She looked extra fine. With mascara on her eyes; it didn't looked as if she broke up with someone.

The boy become serious and the girl broke up? What the fuck is this?

I thought of the boy. He must be crying somewhere; sitting alone in a coffee shop, goggling for Suicide methods like me. He will never come to know that his ex is having fun right now.

'He was childish. He didn't involve much fun. I mean look, he bought me nothing on Valentines. He says he is poor from pocket but rich from heart. I give a damn about his love now, I found someone even better' the girl said again as the other three girls nodded.

Okay, now it's enough.

'What the fuck do you think of yourself?' I shouted, standing up from my table. 'Excuse me?' The girl looked extremely feared with her face red.

'You left him just because he become serious? Is this love? It is because of girls like you we; the boys get fucked over and over again!' I said as I lost balance but thankfully held the table. My condition didn't let me speak so much loudly.

The manager came to my table.

'Sir you are creating a scene here. Security!' He said as in few seconds two guards emerged out of nowhere and kind of threw me out of the coffee shop.

'Fuckers! I paid 120 bucks for my coffee which I didn't even have!' I shouted to the guards as they came near me again.

'Look. Get the fuck out of here! And take this' one of them slapped a hundred rupee note on my face. It hurt me very much. I fell on the floor. In a fraction of seconds, guards disappeared.

I took an auto back to home.

It took me half an hour to reach my home provided how heavy the traffic on the road was. The auto driver charged 200 bucks from me; which was way too much from the normal 150 bucks. Yet; I didn't have the power to fight with him or even speak and handed whatever he wanted.

I knocked the door and after exactly after one hundred and three second, my mom opened it.

Funny how time flies when you are in love but every second counts when you are out of it!

'Beta, will you have lunch?' My mother said. She looked extremely tired. In the past few days; she did all the domestic work by herself with no help from my side.

'No' I said and went to my room, bolting it from inside. I removed my shoes and kept them aside. I changed to my home clothes and sat on the bed; wondering how on earth a simple and good guy likes me can also get screwed by a bitch called 'love'.

To be honest, I was in depression. I didn't talk to anyone. I didn't ate anything, didn't slept. I wanted to commit suicide. I had googled everything on it.

My internet service provider must be shocked at the transition of my internet history from 'Love quotes', 'parallel universe', 'Energy mass equivalence', 'theory of relativity' to 'how to commit suicide without any pain', 'love sucks', 'why it is only the good guy that gets broken every time?'.

I opened my Instagram and saw a bulk of messages there. I ignored all of them. Mostly were from my friends asking me if I were okay now and one from the girl I loved. Or maybe I love.

'Why doesn't she stop texting you now?' The idiot inside me said.

'Maybe because she loves you' the optimist said.

'Ahh, here comes that word again! Love! Had she loved you, she wouldn't have left you like this! She never loved you!' The idiot shouted. His shout rang pain in my head.

'Enough both of you!' I shouted in thin air. I couldn't bear their nonsense anymore. I saw myself in the mirror next to me. **I didn't used to look like this! She did all this to me!**

I opened my course material and started to study.

It was five hours later; when I heard a knock at my door. I opened the door and saw my dad standing there. I looked at the wall clock; it was nine o'clock.

'Mr Malhotra we need to talk' he said. I knew I was in trouble for he called me 'Mr Malhotra' 'Can I come in?'.

'Of course' I said and let him in. Books lied on my bed. He pushed them aside and sat. He signalled me to also sit. I sat next to him.

'Quite busy with these, eh?' He said signalling to the books.

'Yes. Exams are coming' I said.

'Your mother says you have not eaten since three days. Is that true?' He said as at that very instant my stomach clutched and sounded like a whale's mate call.

'Silence speaks it all' he said. 'Why are you doing this to yourself?'

'Doing what?'

'Not taking care of yourself. I know you have exams but this doesn't means that you will turn like this. How is life?' He said. And for the first time in three days, I was talking to someone like this.

'Life is fine. Like it used to be earlier'

'Do you need a counsellor? Therapist?' He said. I looked at him. He was worried about his child's screwed up behaviour.

Do I need a psychiatrist?

'Yes. Would be great if you arrange meeting with one!' I said and fake smiled.

'What is it with your face? Why is it red?' He said as he brought his hand closer to my cheek and touched it. That red spot was due to that bastard guard slapping me.

'Boy you have fever' he said and took out his phone. 'Let's go to the doctor'

'At this time?' I asked puzzled.

'Yes. Wear some jacket. It's cold out there' he said and went out of my room.

'Open your mouth please' the doctor said as he inserted a digital thermometer in my mouth. The doctor had expressions like he was going to say "Congrats, it's a baby boy". My father sat on the sofa next to me. I held the thermometer in mouth for a brief time until he took it out.

'My god, you have got high fever!' He said.

I wanted to slap the doctor and tell him that I just had a breakup!

'What is it with your diet? You look weak and why are you shivering?' He said as he held my hand that was shivering like a Nokia 1100 on vibration mode. My health was really screwed up.

'He doesn't talk with us much. He keeps himself busy' my father said, giving me a *see-what-you-have-done-with-yourself* expression.

The doctor nodded without looking at my father and wrote something on his note pad.

'Here, take these medicines. You will be okay in two three days. Just go and have some food' he said as me and my father stood up to leave.

'And one more thing, you need to visit a psychiatrist. I have a friend, he lives just five minutes from here. He may be free right now' the doctor said handling me the prescription paper and a visiting card. I read it.

Dr S. Mangotra

MBBS, MD Psychiatry

Harvard Medical School

We sat in the car and my dad drove me to the Psychiatrists home. We reached there in five minutes. I saw his home, it was kind of scary.

'I can skip the school and meet him tomorrow!' I said as my dad stopped the car right near his door.

My dad saw my hesitation. I wouldn't be able to discuss my life in front of him, in this much night.

'Okay' he said as he started the engine and started driving to home.

'Good night dad' I said as I bolted my room again from inside. I again was in my own little universe of grief, sorrow, depression and a break up aftermath…

'Sharief…Sharief' I heard a knock at the door while I was again staring at her pics on my phone. I threw my phone aside and went to open the door. It was my mom.

'Go and have a bath. You have a meeting scheduled with a doctor naa? *Shadaiyaan de doctor kol jaana reh gaya hun bas*' she said as I rubbed my eyes. 'Look a little descent. You look like the villains from the 80's. Just shave your beard and have a haircut before you visit him. You are a Punjabi not a Bihari' she said and went into kitchen.

I shaved my beard, got a haircut and went out of the bathroom after a hot shower. I was in a towel. I looked myself in the mirror. My face looked like a tetra pack. The tetra pack that remains after a nine years old child sips whole of his Frooty juice from it. I looked at my wrist, my nerves were now a little visible.

I changed into blue jeans and black shirt and waited for the driver to arrive. In fifteen minutes the driver arrived and he started to drive towards the doctor's home. In another fifteen minutes, we reached there.

I knocked the big door at the threshold of his home. A lady in her mid 30's greeted me and opened the door. She signalled me to go upstairs. I saw him through the transparent glass, sitting in his cabin. His cabin consisted of a sofa and a chair. He sat on the chair.

He saw me and stood.

'Mr Sharief Malhotra?' He said. I expected him to be a little surprised provided it was not my age of visiting a psychiatrist. Yet he seemed normal.

Break ups happen all the time!

'Yes. Good morning doctor' I said recalling his name 'Dr Mangotra'.

He shook hands with me and signalled me to sit on the sofa. I sat, my eyes running through his cabin. It had a rack with books on one side and a television set on the other. It looked as if I had entered an alien world. It was quiet, peaceful and clean.

Maybe I can define infinity now. It is the times the doctor's cabin was clean than my room.

'So what was her name?' He said smiling at me. A shiver ran down my spine suddenly. *What the fuck? How does he know I have had a break up? Is it that much obvious to figure it out?*

'Sorry but how do you know I had a break up?' I said looking straight in his eyes.

'Look. Your parents told me you don't eat, sleep, socialise with them or even laugh. Look at your face, your eyes are swollen. Your face signifies sadness' he said.

'Mahira was her name' I said as I fought a lump in my throat. After exactly three days, eleven hours, fifteen minutes and three seconds, I had mentioned her name.

'Mahira. Nice name' he said.

'What do you want to hear? You know that she left me and I am alone now. What else?' I asked as tears appeared in my eyes ready to shoot.

'I want to know the whole thing from start' he said 'Only then I will be able to figure it out' he said.

'Before starting I want to make some revelations' I said.

'Okay. Carry on'

'I drank for the first time after she left me' I said looking down. It was something I will be guilty of till I die, 'I guess this is what you do when you think you will die…'

'And?' The doctor said, his expression normal and calm as ever, smiling.

'My heart has been broken twice. There was a girl before too' I said and literally he let out a laughter.

See! Even the psychiatrist laughs at you!

'Sorry but I don't think it is funny' I said.

'No. No…It's not funny. You just remind me of myself. You know what, when I was your age I was rejected five times' he said, 'funny how we let love fuck us every time even though we know it will give us pain in the end.'

'Yes. Love is the only thing that fucks all of us over and over again but still doesn't give us AIDS' I said and he laughed.

'Okay. So start from the beginning…' he said.

'It starts in September. When I started to love her, more than anyone.'

'Hey sorry to interrupt you but would you like to have some food?' he said, 'my wife makes very good food.'

'Okay, I will' I said as he smiled and picked his phone to maybe text his wife. In a few minutes, his wife or the lady that greeted me at the door came in the cabin with two plates full of boiled vegetables. She left after placing them on the table.

'Garden salad. I love it' he said as he started eating his salad. I picked up mine and played a little with the veggies before starting to eat.

'Okay. So as I said, it started in September. When the girl whom I loved had her birthday and the girl whom I love well she was yet to come in my life' I said with my mouth stuffed....

I

I stood outside the class and looked at the small print out pasted on the door that read '6th C'.

The teacher was yet to come. I kept standing outside and staring the door, fearing the world behind it. They say you kind of become mature when you come in sixth class. I showed no sign of maturity. No beard, no moustache, no sweaty armpits, no sweaty palms and no attraction towards any girl. When my friends played girlish games with their girl-friends, I buried my nose in a book and getting lost in it like there was no such thing as 'reality' and 'fiction' was all that existed!

Let me introduce myself to you. I am Sharief Malhotra. I am dumb, average heightened and ugly. Yes, I am ugly and I have accepted it. It's not something that I can hold grudges for a lot of time. I have a below average face that looks like Voldemort had an affair with Rakhi Sawant when I remove my glasses I am good at um....er...nothing. When I say 'nothing' I mean 'nothing'.

I am that person who searches 'How to make Maggie' on Google. Useless, dumb and idiot are like the perfect synonyms for me.

After consistently coming second in the last three classes, here I am in sixth standard. Our school has a screwed up policy in which they shuffle kids in sixth standard. This means that all the friends I made (from all I mean only two, Dhananjay and Divi) had to go away from me. I wanted to slap on the face of the bastard who made such policy. Sometimes, you and your friends get shuffled in the same class. I prayed to god last night for them to stay with me. They were my best friends, yes they were.

'Beta, why are you standing outside?' I heard a female voice from behind as a hand landed on my shoulder. I turned to her. Mrs Geetanjali, one of the best Hindi teacher of our school stood there.

I smiled at her. She looked just like my mother. She opened the door and all the noise coming from the other side stopped in an instant!

I entered the class and looked at the kids sitting in the front. My eyes scanned for the two idiots. I wasn't able to find them. A quick scan of my class made me realised it was full of the most fashion conscious kids of the school. My eyes suddenly shifted to the last bench and it brought a huge smile on my face.

Dhananjay and Divi sitting on the last bench, waving at me and high fiving each other. Divi was the taller one among us and Dhananjay was the shorter one. We three had nothing in common. Dhananjay's dad was in Power Grid Department, mine in National Sample Survey and Divi's in Punjab National Bank. Maybe it was the middle class background or the repetition of 'pickle' and 'mix veg' in our lunch box that held us together.

I waved at them and started to walk towards the last bench.

'Beta' I heard the teacher say again from behind. I turned to her and she stared me like I was the younger brother of E.T.

'Sit in front' she said pointing to the desk in the front. A girl was already sitting on it.

'But mam…they are my frien…' I said as she cut me mid way.

'Sixth standard demands hard work, time, patience. Not friendships. You are grown up now beta. Concentrate on your studies' she said and smiled. I frowned and sat on the front desk next to the unknown girl.

I had never talked to a girl in my whole life, let alone the thing of sitting next to one.

'All set class?' she asked.

'Yes mam' the class said in unison.

'Okay, so we need to introduce ourself don't we. I am Geetanjali, your Hindi teacher for the year and your class teacher too!' she said and blushed. She looked extremely cute. 'Now one by one stand up on your seat and introduce yourself.'

It took twenty minutes for fifteen kids to introduce themselves until my turn came.

I stood up.

'Mam, my name is Sharief Malhotra and I love reading books' I said and sat again.

It was her turn now. The unknown girl. I didn't even bothered to look at her even once because I had no interest in her. Not that I am gay but I never looked at girls that way. I was too much busy with my studies and all that I never had the time to even think about a girl.

I looked at her. Believe me, she was beautiful! She was long, slender, white with her eyes blue. It looked like that she just came out from a Disney fairy tale book! She looked like an angel.

'Good morning mam. My name is Mohini Sharma. My hobbies are listening to music and reading fiction novels. I am looking forward to study well under your guidance this year mam' she said and smiled. The teacher blushed and the whole class burst into whispers. I could literally hear every boy whispering about her to the next person.

Huh! Ass kisser! Looking forward to work under your guidance! Hahaha!

I couldn't tolerate to sit with this *typical ass kissing girl* for the rest of the year!

I thought of plans to get my seats changed. My plans ranged from puking at her to telling her that I am HIV positive to stripping in front of her. After a lot of calculations, I excluded the last one from the list.

'Hi' she said and extended her hand towards me. She looked pure innocent, cute and lovable!

'Hi' I said and shook hands with trembling fingers. Holding her hands sent a current down my spine. It was the first physical contact I had ever had with a female. She smiled.

'I am sorry but I think I should tell you that I am HIV positive' I lied in an attempt to get my seat changed.

She came a little more near me and smiled.

'It's okay. I have read it on the internet. HIV spreads only when you sleep with each other. It's a sexually transmitted disease not a physically transmitted one. We are cool' she said.

DAMN! SHIT!

'How can you say that word?' I said, feeling a little insecure on the choice of her words at the age of twelve.

'Which word?' she said, as innocent as always.

'The S...word' I whispered as low as possible.

'What? Sex? It is common isn't it? We are here because of it. Why hide from the fact. India has one billion populations and it is clear that all of them didn't fell from above!' she said like she was in a debate.

They say there are some moments when you immediately start liking someone and believe me, this was it!

I stared at her face. She looked far beautiful from the girls I had ever imagined! The glittery big blue eyes on her face were like the icing on the cake! I didn't want to get my seat changed anymore. I wanted to sit with her for lifetime, forever, till the world ends!

'Are you new in school? Never seen you before' I said pulling the chain of the train of my thoughts.

'Actually we were in the same class last year too. I know you won't remember because every time I saw you, you were studying some book or the other. You hardly talked to anyone. Is it because of the HIV thing? I can convince everyone if you want me to' she said. Little explosions lighted my mind and I laughed.

'Hey, why are you laughing?' she said with her eyebrows shot up. Girls look even more beautiful when angry!

'I am sorry but I lied to you…I just wanted to get my seat changed. That's all. I never wanted to be friend with a girl but you seem like a nice girl…' I said and she frowned.

'It's okay' she said. A wide grin appeared on my face while looking at her.

'What?' she said looking at my lost expressions.

'Nothing…You…are…Beautiful' I stammered.

'Seriously? I am ugly!' she protested.

'No! I am ugly! Look at me' I said. She shook her head.

'You are cute' she said and smiled. I blushed like a tomato. It was the first ever compliment I had ever got from a girl. Or maybe it was the first compliment by someone ever!

By that time, all the students had done introducing themselves and the teacher was again in her usual *teaching* mode.

'Okay so class, this will be the seating arrangement for the rest of the year too. I hope you study well and do the homework on time. And dare to change your seat' she warned as the class nodded. The first sentence said by her made my day. If I had a Swiss bank account, I would have transferred all my money to her account for that!

The teacher started teaching. Unintentionally, her arm touched mine and I liked this little contact of ours. We studied together and worked as hard as possible to find the answers to the question the teacher had given us. We would discuss our answers before speaking them out.

She was different from other girls though I didn't know any other girl but I feel this. She was like Sharief Malhotra in a female body. We liked the same books, the same movies, the same authors. It was a phenomenon experience that day.

The bell rang and it was recess time. Unlike every day, I kept sitting there with her when I could have gone with Dhananjay and Divi to play and share my lunch with them. She told me to pass her bag and I picked her pink 'Barbie' doll bag and passed it to her. I grinned at her. She was still childish but mature too at the same time. She took out a small purple lunch box out of it and I took out mine. My lunch box was not a lunch box. It was a used 'Amul butter' transparent container that was turned into a lunch box by my mother. No one does better recycling than a middle class family!

I opened it and it was the usual pickle and chapatti for me. I offered her and she took whole of it like she never ate pickle before in her whole life. I rolled my eyes at her. She gave me her lunch. It was paneer cooked in rich red gravy with two chapattis without butter. I ate one of it in one go.

'You must be rich' I hardly managed to speak with my mouth full.

'No. What makes you say so?' she said, still eating my lunch.

'You brought paneer. This fancy bag, lunch box and all. You must be quite rich' I said highlighting my observation.

'So? I bring paneer so I am rich? I am not. I am middle class' she said.

I regretted asking her this question. It must have hurt her.

'Who else is in your family?' I asked her in an attempt to change the topic.

'Umm...My mother, father and a little sister!' she said.

'Same here!'

'Oh! So you also have a nuclear family?' she asked me.

'Yours must be a nuclear family. Mine is a nuclear bomb' I said and she burst into laughter.

'Is your father a businessman?' I asked. *Middle class can never be friends with upper class. They can only be their minions!*

'No...My dad's a government officer and mom's a housewife' she said.

I literally jumped from my seat. *How can two people have so many similarities?*

'What happened?' she asked holding my arm. It felt like a naked wire with thousand volt current touching my body.

'How can we have so many similarities? My dad's a government officer too, an IAS to be precise' I said as her eyes widened as if she got to knew that I was really HIV positive.

'Don't tell me! IAS? Your dad? Oh my god!' she exclaimed with a huge surprised smile.

I found the news of my dad being an IAS as boring as the history teacher's lecture. There was nothing to be excited about.

'Yes. Is it a shocker?'

'Of course idiot it is! Oh my god! It was my dream to meet an IAS officer and guess what, I am friend of one's son!' she said as she sat back on her seat and removed her hand from my arm.

'Leave it. You know...' I said as I saw some students from the adjacent class peeping inside through the window. I glared at them and they backed off.

'I don't think we should be friends. Look these kids...They keep staring you. You are like the most beautiful girl in the world and I am a typical nerd. A nerd who has nothing to do but study.

You yourself know how much I kept myself involved with studies and all. I…' I said and she cut me mid way.

'Come with me' she said and stood up from her seat. I followed her outside the room where those random kids who were peeping inside the class a moment ago stood.

'Hey guys!' she said as if she already knew each one of them.

'Hell…Hello' said the three, stammering.

'See frankly speaking I don't know who you are but as I can see, you guys are humans right?' she said, her blue eyes glittering.

I kept staring her face with my mouth open. She looked perfectly beautiful.

'Yes. We are humans!' one of them said more shouted.

'Oh, that's great! You see, the best trait of a good human is to mind his own business. Why the hell were you staring both of us huh?' she said as Dhananjay emerged out of the class to participate in *World War III*.

'Hey, we are sor…Sorry. We didn't mean to stare inside. We were just looking inside!' another said as the other two hung their head in shame.

'You better be. And remember, the next time you again peep inside the class, I will tell his father. He's an IAS officer and can get your even your last two generations jailed' she said pointing to me. I nodded.

'Are you two a couple?' the guy who was quiet till now asked.

'Only if it matters. Yes!' she snapped as she left the crime scene leaving me and Dhananjay behind.

'What the f…' he said and poked my stomach.

I stood there motionless. Are we really a couple? Is she also in love with me? Are we boy friend and girl friend?

'You never told me! Bastard' he said. I shook my head still thinking.

Okay, so this is what had happened in the past few hours. I am forced to sit with an unknown girl who turns out to be my last year's classmate too but talk to her for the first time today. She has got all these blue eyes, fairy complexion, excellent verbal things and a damn mature soul. I kind of fall in love or maybe start liking her, we discuss things that unintentionally or by fate turns out to be similar and suddenly, here she is telling those random bastards that 'we are a couple'! Like how is this even possible? I have never been attracted to a girl so much in my whole life because the only girls I knew until today were either in my family or the female characters of the fictional novels I read!

I walked in the class quietly and saw her reading a book. Her face could be the perfect example for 'furious'. Anger and hormones must have been raging through her face because it looked 'red'. Redder than mine, when she had said that I was cute!

I sat next to her quietly and stared at her. She kept looking hard in the book, maybe trying to ignore me.

What have I done? Why are we not talking? We are a 'couple' right? Though we just met few hours ago, we are couple. Right?

'Hey, what happened?' I asked as she breathed heavily.

'You know it very well...' she hissed in an angry tone. Her blue eyes turned little shades of red.

Is it because of that couple thing?

'No...I don't' I said.

'You could have smashed their faces. They were staring us. But what did you do? Kept standing there, open mouthed. Are you really a boy?' she said and again dug her nose in the book.

'Hey. Look at me' I said and took that book from her. She protested a little but finally gave it to me. I kept it aside.

'You see, when a dog bites you, you don't bite back! When a terrorist bombs you, you don't bomb his city back! Just like that when a stalker stalks you or stares at you, just ignore them. Those boys are going through their puberty. Their hormones rage, they need some material to fant…Sorry think about! Like a really beautiful girl. When a beautiful and intelligent girl like you gets into a fight with them, they get the message that they have won. They lose when we ignore them. Boys will be boys. This is just a small school and the start of the sixth standard. Don't you think you have to go through infinite such stares in your life, pass through numerous tests, and hear comments on your appearance because you are a female. It's not an IAS who should make them scared but your own power. Power of being a female! I am also a boy but trust me, I never objectified women. They only have one role in my life, the role of being a mere competitor. This doesn't means that I am gay or not a boy. I respect girls. I am not of the believe that staring girls will make me a little more manly. Do you get my point?' I said from my little brain which I expected only churned mono syllables till now. I don't know how I said this all but I really said this.

She looked at me, lost. A wide smile appeared on her face and I fell blue lights on my face from her eyes. She kept staring at me. I felt a little insecure.

'You heard what I said?' I asked her, placing my hand on her shoulder.

'Um…Yes' she said and smiled again. The smile was idiotic, worse than mine!

She first nodded then shook her head and looked at me.

'You are a really nice guy. I am sorry for whatever I said. I am just sorry…' she said as the bell rang and the class returned.

Not a single word was exchanged between us later that day. Though I didn't talked about it, I kept repeating that phrase of her in my mind a thousand times.

'Only if it matters… Yes, we are a couple!'

II

Mohini Sharma

Whoa!! What was that!

I sat in the car and smiled again. His words repeated in my mind again and again. All his words exactly. Like I had got them recorded! I didn't even miss a single word. His words made me feel a little more secure, safe and beautiful too.

'How was the first day princess?' the superhero of my life, my dad asked me as I pulled seat belt on.

'It was amazing dad!' I said and hugged him as tight as possible. We, the daughters share a special, complex yet fun relation with our dad. Only the two know about it. People may talk about 'Mama's boy' but 'Daddy's princess' sounds much better to me.

'Made some new friends?' he asked, smiling.

'Yes' I said and blushed.

Why am I blushing? Have I completely lost it?

'What's his name?' he said as he pressed the horn in the huge traffic outside the school.

What? How does he knows that?

'His name? What are you talking dad?' I said and shook my head. I struggled to keep a straight face. The face of an intelligent feminist.

'I am your dad. I know everything, princess' he said.

What am I going to tell him?

'Okay, so here it goes. I met a really cute guy. Like he was really cute. Far cute than even a teddy bear. He is into the same things as me. He too got a small family like us. His dad is an IAS! Imagine! He's far intelligent than me, don't know why he keeps calling himself 'ugly'. I called him gay for he didn't uttered even a single word when some random kids from the next class were staring us and now I regret that. He told me some things. Things that made the feminist inside me a little more powerful. He said that I will have to go through a lot of shitty things like this. Many stares, comments on my appearance and all. His words were amazing. Though some of his logic of 'biting back a dog' and 'bombing a terrorist's city back' sucked but still…I think I kind of like him. And I think he likes me too. He was open mouthed all the time I was shattering the ego of those bastard kids who were staring at me! Yep, that's the truth' I could have said that but I don't think it's the right time to tell him this.

Sixth has just started and I have many more things to concentrate on rather than just 'Sharief Malhotra'. I giggled when his name came in my thought.

'There's no *he* in my life other than you dad! The day that *he* will come, you'll be the first one to hear about him!' I said and smiled.

'First one? Even before Natasha and Divya? You must be kidding me!' he said.

This is when it hit me hard. Natasha and Divya were my best friends since first standard and we are in the same class this year too (though they were absent). What will they think about him? What if they laugh at me? What if they don't like him?

I made a face as the car came to a stop. We were home.

'Hey, I didn't meant to hurt you' he said as he unbuckled his seat belt.

'Who told you I am hurt? We are rolling! Yes, even before them' I said and unbuckled mine.

I got out of my car and saw mom sitting on the sofa as usual, watching 'Saas vs Bahu' episode infinity!

'I am home' I said as I put my bag on the other sofa and sat next to her. She came near me and kissed on my cheek.

'Mera beta' she said. Indian parents sometimes call their daughter 'beta'. I don't know if it's because they want to convince themselves that they have a son not a daughter or if they really love us, but in my case the reason is surely the latter one!

'How was the first day of sixth, young lady?' she said and winked.

Young lady was an internal joke between only me and my mom. I had started getting periods just last month and it was then when I told my mother about the bleeding and the need for sanitary pads. Since then, she calls me a 'Young lady'. Sometimes even dad laughs at this jokes of ours but later makes a straight face. It's kind of embarrassing to imagine that your mom has told your dad about your periods.

I don't think Sharief will think the same about female power if he one day gets periods. The imagination of this situation made me laugh out loud.

My mother looked shockingly at me.

'What?' she said.

'This old lady, what's her name...Saasu maa still hasn't died even after infinite episodes and numerous leaps. Like how's this even possible' I said pointing towards the television which still played that shitty serial with a shitty plot. I don't really know how the writers of these shows don't get embarrassed while telling someone that they write this. Its pure shit.

'That's so rude of you' she said, 'so as I was asking you something, how was your day?'

'Damn amazing!' I said and managed not to grin.

'Go, change and have some lunch' she said. I shook my head. It felt like those pickle and buttered chapattis were still in the upper part of my food pipe.

'I am not hungry. I need some sleep. That's it' I said and stood up to leave for my room.

'As you wish, young lady' she said. I went inside my room and bolted the door. I sat on the bed and started thinking of how to apologize to Sharief for calling him gay. It was surely a dick move. He must have been hurt. He's so kind. Why did I snapped at him? Puberty hit girls bad. Our hormones make us either happy as hell or angry as fuck. There's no in-between.

'You are a bad bad girl Mohini' I mumbled to myself. Suddenly an idea popped in my mind. I can write a short poem to apologize to him. He'll surely like it.

I picked up a notebook and started scribbling a poem on it with my pencil.

I am sorry for I called you gay

I was angry *and that was all I could say*

I have realised that Boys fighting is too main stream

Your words were flattening and more appealing than some whipped coffee cream

Whatever you said, I know it's true

You are a nice guy and I think I like you!

I cut the last two lines and throw the whole paper in the bin. I don't think it's the right time to tell him that I really like him. It's been just one day with him. The poem was gross. Even a three years own could have written better!

I heard a knock at the door.

'Mohini…Beta' my mother shouted from the other side.

I stood up and opened the door. She stood there, smiling.

Frankly, I have a girl crush on my mom.

'What are you doing' She asked, 'you still haven't changed. What's it?'

'Um...Nothing' I said. Sweat beads started to appear on my face. My face muscles twitched.

'Why are you so tensed?' She said.

The worst thing with girls is that we can't hide our secrets even if we try our best. Our body language automatically changes when we are in our 'shhh! We have a secret' mode.

'I am getting cramps' I lied. I couldn't think of anything else at that time.

'Oh...baccha' she placed her hand on my face, 'do you want to consult the doctor? Dr Gupta?'

Dr Gupta was our family gynaecologist. She had done my as well as my younger sister's delivery.

My mother had made me meet her when I got my periods. She told me useless things. I might be grateful to her for bringing me in this screwed up world, but the way she tried to counsel me was ridiculous.

I shook my head in horror.

'No mom. I am okay with it!' I said.

'Are you sure?' She said, her expressions more serious than mine.

'Yes maa' I said and smiled.

'Mera baccha...Bada ho gaya hai ab...mummy se baatein chupaata hai" she said and kissed me on my cheek.

She disappeared back into the kitchen and I change into my home clothes.

I sat on the bed and opened my course material. I started to study and revise whatever we had been taught today. With every question, his voice appeared in my head.

"Do it like this…You do silly mistakes" he had said.

I smiled. I made up my mind of apologizing to him tomorrow. He must be feeling sad and hurt. How could I be so mean?

After three more hours, I heard a knock at the door. It was my mom again.

'Here, I bought these for you…The days are close naa?' she said and handed me something wrapped in a newspaper. They were the sanitary pads.

Okay, so you people talk about equality. Where the hell do your equality goes when you sell something like sanitary pads wrapped in a newspaper while drugs and alcohol are sold as it is.

Don't these shopkeepers realise that its something related with genetics? So what if we bleed? Does it means you are going to sell us the things we need wrapped in newspapers so that nobody can see what we are going through? Is it a crime?

I made a face the moment I saw the wrapping of a newspaper.

'Maa…I have told you ample of times that you don't need to get this covered in a newspaper!' I snapped.

'Beta…We need to maintain a space between our personal and private life. We need to create a barrier between how we see ourselves and how our family sees us' she said.

'Why is it always the girls who get screwed in this whole process? Why do only the females need to create a fake image of themselves in front of their family? You change the channel whenever some commercial of whisper or god knows which ever brand comes. And here you are, holding that in your hand' I said, angrier than ever.

'It's a girl thing. You will slowly understand it…Shobha's daughter's reception is today. You decided what you'll be wearing?' she said.

'Shorts?' I said and laughed out loud.

She shook her head in horror and told me to change as soon as possible.

I opened my cupboard and saw infinite clothes in there. I still don't believe how I say, "Mom I have no clothes" whenever I have to go to a party!

I picked them out randomly and threw them aside.

This is also why being female sucks. We have to balance between being called an 'aunty' and being called a 'slut'. There's a thin line which is as thin as a hair that separates the two. Wear small clothes you are slut, characterless, whore. Wear long clothes you are aunty, ancient, old fashioned. Making this balance is more difficult than balancing a thousand gram mass on one side of the see saw and a one gram mass on the other!

After thirty five minutes, I found the perfect dress. It was a pink stellar dress. I thanked god for I had the matching heels with it too.

I dressed into it and applied a light kohl and a light pink lipstick. I checked myself about fifty times in the mirror, thanks to the *"Log kya kahenge"* (What will people say) phenomena.

My room had surely turned into a graveyard of clothes. All my dresses lied in different corners. I knew that it could get me scolded from mom but still, I wasn't in the mood of cleaning my room.

I got out of my room and saw my mother, sitting on the sofa watching another lame serial dressed in a light green saree. Had she participated in any of the fashion pageant of the world, she would have easily won it.

'Maa. When will you stop watching these shitty serials!' I said and sat next to her. She smiled.

'The day when my daughter stops looking like the world's most beautiful girl' she said and I blushed.

Mothers are the best flirt in the world!

'I am not the most beautiful girl. You are' I said and hugged her hard.

At that moment I heard footsteps and a few seconds later, I saw my younger sister standing in front of us.

'Aisha...You look stunning' I said. She was wearing a red bodycon dress.

'Ohoo...Beautiful ladies' my dad said from behind.

'Someone's looking really smart' my mom said. He smiled.

'Thank you so much honey!' he said. He wore his traditional *It's a family function* clothes.

'I am talking about Shah Rukh, honey' mom said as she pointed to the TV which played a commercial with Shah Rukh in it.

All four of us burst into laughter.

'Lets go' dad said as we sat in our car and he started to drive.

Twenty minutes later, we reached 'Triple S farms'. DJ played music at highest level possible. I imagined what would have been the condition of the people in here if the 'S' in the name is replaced by a 'X'.

I saw over dressed people standing outside. Few men wearing pink turbans. Well those pink turbans are a kind way of telling others that "We payed for it all. Eat little please!".

We got out of the car. Though I recognised no one, pleasantries and Namaste's were exchanged between me and random people.

As we entered the hall, I let out a laugh. I saw Shobha aunty's daughter and son-in-law sitting on a couch like zombies and getting pictures clicked as if they were some kind of celebrities!

We went on the stage and dad gave the shagun to the bride. Both of them seeked my parent's blessings and we got a picture clicked with them.

I saw some random retired uncles dancing to old beats on the dance floor. They probably were drunk.

'Dii. How can they dance on such a rubbish song?' Aisha asked.

'They are drunk right now. They can even dance to the sound of a generator' I said and she laughed.

Like all the middle class families, we split in the food stalls to avoid being looked together and suspected of eating more.

I picked up a plate and went to the aloo tiki stall. The crowd at the stall could be mistaken as some best selling author's book signing from a distance.

'Haath hi daal lo' the guy who was frying the tikkis told to the old man who just had his hand a centimeter away from the pan.

I looked at other stalls and saw a familiar figure having pani puri. It was him. Sharief Malhotra.

Like Tom Cruise from mission impossible movies, I sneaked right behind him without being caught. He gulped the pani puris like he was from some famine affected area.

After twenty more, he threw the disposable plate right near the cardboard box that was supposed to be the dustbin. I wanted to slap him for he didn't even cared to dispose the waste right.

I maintained some distance from him and he went to the plate counter to get himself another plate.

He went to the Dosa stall now. I was mentally laughing at his condition. Don't his parents give him food?

'Bhaiya…It's for two people. Please give a little more' he said as the person on the stall dumped his plate twice with the *Made in China* Dosa. He went away from the stall, a considerable distance where no one could see him.

I followed him. He looked somewhere, probably at the Dosa guy and after a few seconds, started having it all by him!

Liar bastard!

'You are such a liar...and so hungry' I said as his Dosa laced hand froze in air. He turned back to me and smiled.

He wore a dark blue T shirt and jeans which made him look a little smarter than how he looks in the school.

'Mohini' he said and brought his hand towards me.

'No way. You got this cheap dosa all over your hands' I said and shook my head.

'Oh sorry' he said and took out his handkerchief, rubbing the living hell out of his hand.

'How come are you here?' we said in unison and laughed.

'Shoba's my aunty' I said.

'Oh...I am from the boy's side!' he said. I smiled.

'Hey...I wanted to say something' I said as his eyes widened.

'Y...Yes yes' he said stammering. Maybe he likes me too.

'I am sorry' I said looking down.

He put his hand on my shoulder.

'For what?' he said.

'For I called you gay today...In school'

'Are you serious? I even forgot about it. You girls naa' he said and smiled.

'You are looking stunningly beautiful and amazing by the way' he said and I blushed.

'You said you never objectify women!' I joked.

'Okay. You look ugly' he said. I made a face and he laughed.

'I am joking...' he said.

'Let's eat something. I am damn hungry' I said and made a puppy face.

'Take this' he said as he handed me a plate and picked up one for himself too.

We ate a lot together. I had never eaten so much before. Maybe sometimes only we need the right company to be ourselves, right?

III

The friendship between me and Mohini kept growing stronger and stronger day by day. We shared our lunches, we discussed the books we read, and we did endless chit chats together.

She was the first girl ever I felt so much emotionally attached to. In one word, she was my 'life'. People around me were jealous because frankly, we didn't had a match. Even as a friend.

I kept thinking about her all the time. My life became a roller coaster. They were the happiest days of my life. Sometimes she would ask me if I liked any girl. I just shook my head or to put it straight, 'lied'.

I googled 'I like my best friend. Is it normal?'. The results boosted my moral. Yes, it was normal. Though I should have searched 'I love my best friend'.

My grades stepped on a banana peel. All my time was either wasted in looking a little handsome or thinking and talking to her. I never told my parents about her. The reaction a Punjabi family gives when you tell them your best friend is a girl is same as the reaction a Catholic gives on teenage pregnancy!

Our talks were only limited to school hours. She didn't had a Smartphone neither did I. But as they say, even God helps love sometimes, it was on her thirteenth birthday she got a phone from her parents. And so did I!

She told me to download the social networking app 'Whatsapp'. Things turned out to be real sweet. We exchanged our numbers and she had warned me to give anyone else her contact (unless she tells me to).

After analysing the situation a little, I thought that she considered me 'SAFE'. Yes, the word that is particularly used for friend zoned guys. 'SAFE' guys are those who are the only have the limit of being a best friend of a girl. Nothing more. It was funny that though I knew somewhere I was kind of friend zoned, still I felt I should work my ass off to make her love me.

Unfortunately, Love isn't forceable. You can do a few bad things to make someone hate you but in the case of 'love', it's not like that!

I was confused as hell. I knew I never deserved her even as a friend let alone the thing of us being in a relation. But she was the first love of my life. The first true love, for which I could stand in storms, float in lava and all those utter impossible shit lovers talk about.

She told me that I was the only guy she talked for so long. I sent her jokes, songs, shayaries, whatever I could do to bring a smile on her face. She liked me, she had admitted this.

The truth was never hidden from me though. She was literally out of my league.

These three years had brought quite some changes in me. I became a little taller, with facial hair exploding on my face and hormones raging like never before.

I had lost quite some weight. Well, from quite some weight I mean transformation from a triple chinned guy to a single chinned guy. I had stopped having all those junk and shit that I used to have all this time. Eventually, a little exercise also made things great.

Even though so with many changes, I was still the fat guy with teeth that were stained with yellow a little and who wore spectacles. On the other hand, she still was the same Mohini Sharma.

The tall, lean, fair and blue eyed girl that had stole my heart the moment I saw her.

The thought to tell her that I liked her kept dominating my mind. I had read somewhere, "Hearts are left broken because of words left unspoken".

Though when we talked normally, we behaved like we were friends but whenever the issue of 'love' or 'crush' came up, I talked to her like a guy having his both the balls in mouth!

One such day, I gathered enough courage to tell her that I liked her. Well, I didn't straight away told her that I liked her.

My plan wasn't to bend on my knees and give her a rose telling her that I love her and will love her even after the world ends (this was what I really wanted to do), I instead sent her the trending romantic song of that time, *'Mera Mann Kehne Laga'*. I hoped she would understand that I was a dick and didn't had the courage of telling my best girl-friend that I loved her and would keep her happy for the rest of the life!

My phone bleeped just seconds later after I sent her the song.

I opened the message, with my heart beating unusually fast.

"Why did you sent this song to me? :D"

What the fuck? Can't she see that I love her? Can't she see that everything I did till now, was to make her happy ? Is she playing a little with me?

"Hahaha! There's nothing like that! A boy sent me that song so what do you think, the boy…It's a nice song naa?" I mumbled while typing and sent her.

"Hahahha. Yeah! That song is sooo romantic *_*"

I threw my phone away. I was literally an idiot. I couldn't tell the girl I loved that I loved her! How stupid was that! Love makes us idiot though I already was one.

Things changed when another guy came into her life. He told her that he loved her, would count starts for her, would even put Neil Armstrong to shame by bringing down the moon at her feet, everything I wanted to say. Though I don't want to take his name, he was rich. Quite rich. He could afford the expenses of my coming three generations all at once.

I started hearing rumours about her. Rumours that said she was in a secret relation with that guy. Though that guy was rich and all, I admit that he wasn't as smart as me. He was literally an idiot who built his body in gym. Flunking and fucking were his main pass times. Mohini, being my best friend had told me that there was nothing between them though her friends, seemed a little more excited about that guy.

The rumour mill was all over the school. People started to question her character and my friends warned me to stay away from her if I wanted to do it some good in my life. I was angry as hell from all of them. I had stopped talking to all my friends.

Rumours are a dick move. They are created by people weaker than you who are jealous of you. Ultimately, they end up destroying a perfectly happy life.

'Do you really trust them Sharief?' she asked me as she wiped tears off her beautiful face. Those blue eyes cried and it hurt me! We sat on our desk, together like the past four years.

'No…I trust you Mohini…I am your friend…I will always be there for you' I said. Her face brightened up. Though I never objectified women, I just wanted to kiss her! Yes, I had turned quite a little pervertish in these years.

'Why is everyone so rude with me? Why can't they see there is nothing like that' she said, 'I am just friends with him and he likes me. There's nothing else. NOTHING' she said with her perfect lips. I shifted in my seat for I didn't want to get jailed for molestation charges on my best friend.

'Time will heal everything girl...This is nothing' I said and held her hand. Only boys can help girls through their bad times, admit it!

I heard heavy footsteps and shifted my vision as Diveesh, one of my *best friends whom I had stopped talking to for they believed in the rumours* came near to our desk. I stood up.

'Hey Sharief!' he said. I rolled my eyes at him.

'See. You made our brother chutiya. She screwed you man' he said and glared at her.

'Please Diveesh. I don't have the power to fight with anyone right now' she said.

'Yes. How could you have the power and stamina to fight? Last night must have been tiring isn't it? Which guy did you slept with huh?' he said as I stood up.

'What shit are you talking Diveesh!...' I said as he cut me mid sentence.

'SHE IS A BITCH! A FUCKING SLUT! SHE USED YOU! FORWARDED THOSE SHAYARIES YOU SENT HER TO THAT MOTHERFUCKER!' he shouted angrily as he spat on the ground.

'What the hell?' I said and looked at him, Mohini behind me.

'Get a side; let me teach her a lesson. She fucked your life!' he said and pushed me. Being way too much short, his push had no effect on me. I stood there, glaring and staring at his eyes.

Before I could even do something, a tight slap landed on Mohini's face. That son of a bitch had slapped her. He had slapped the love of my life. How dare that motherfucker!

Her cheeks became red as a small red mark of his short fingers appeared on her face. She cried. Tears flowed at unstoppable pace. She sobbed.

'YOU ASSHOLE' I clenched my fist and punched right into his face. My fist being big had quite effect on him. Blood flowed from his face faster than the tears Mohini had just shed. He fell on the floor.

My two best friends, Dhananjay and Divi rushed to me and held me before I could have slapped and punched and kicked that bastard some more!

'You slapped your best friend for a girl? A fucking girl that has maybe slept with infinitely many guys! You call me your friend huh?' he said, still lying on the floor, blood still rushing out of his face.

'Mind your words motherfucker. She is not like that. She is my best friend. How dare you touch her?' I shouted.

He waved a middle finger to her. I saw her. She was expressionless and pale. She stood there like time had just stopped for her. She showed no moment.

'Mohini?' I said to her. She looked into my eyes and kept staring me with those same zombie like expressions.

'Mohini…you okay?' I said as a tear fell from her eye and she hugged me hard. It was like one of the best feelings ever. Hugging your crush. She sobbed as she tightened her grip around me. Others in the class were still to recover from what had just happened.

'Everything's okay' I said and rubbed her head. I felt her tears on my shirt.

'Hey, look at me' I told to her and she lifted her face. The right cheek was still swelled up.

'Thank you Sharief…Thank you so much' she said and smiled. The cheeks turned pinkish and the lips red.

My mind calculated the number of Diveesh I would need to punch in order to make her kiss me. Punch one, she hugs. Maybe if I punch two…

This is the sickness of a male mind. No matter how serious the situation is, it somehow manages to add sex to it!

After that incident, things had quite changed. Nobody spoke shit about her now. Everyone now was aware that there was a guy named 'Sharief Malhotra' who could screw the living shit out of anyone if it comes to Mohini.

My relations with my mother became worse. Well, I blame myself for it. The raging hormones can make you do anything...I won't like to talk about that now.

Mohini and I had bonded up more strongly. She knew I was her side and trusted me blindly. I made a list of boys who didn't seemed safe to me and warned Mohini not to talk to them. To my surprise, she seriously stopped talking to those boys.

"Why aren't you talking to me?" they would ask sometimes.

"Sharief told me not to" she would reply with a hint of pride in her smile.

How cute!

I attempted many a times again to tell her that I liked her. But seeing the situation, I later turned them into a 'prank' for being easily edible for both of us. The fear of our friendship being lost constantly invaded my mind.

It was the last day on ninth I made up my mind to tell her my feelings.

I woke up at four of the morning. I did few push ups and sit ups. It felt like I was going on a war. A war where the only thing at stake was our friendship.

I stood in front of the mirror and practiced infinitely about how it would be easy for me to tell her the truth. Though I considered myself a writer, all my verbal skills had vanished right now. I stood in front of mirror and looked in my own eyes.

'I love you MMM...Mohini' I said like Shah Rukh Khan with my arms wide open. I looked like a monkey!

I applied a perfume for the first time in my life. I was of the thought that the people who don't bath are the one who apply perfume and I showered daily. Though it was my mother's ladies perfume, I hoped it would hide my shyness in front of her.

I touched the feet of my parents and left for the school. It was now or never. I bought a small chocolate from the market on the way and got it wrapped in a blue packing paper with a note attached to it.

Dear Mohini,

Let me get things straight. I love you. Yes, I really love you. Though I had never admitted it in front of you, my mind only thinks about you. Your blue eyes are just adorable. I love your lips, your eyes, your face, your smile or I think I should put it like this, I simply love 'you'. I know I am an idiot, I don't have the courage to tell you this face to face. It feels like I have my balls in my mouth when I talk to you. I am way too much shy. I love you, I love you, I love you. You are beautiful and I have told my friends that you really are!!!!

Yours
Sharief Malhotra

P.S: Sorry for the melted chocolate. The shopkeeper didn't had a fridge.

P.P.S: Sorry for my handwriting too :D

I had written this note just last night on a page torn from my rough notebook. The words were exaggerating if looked from a neutral point of view but still, I hoped she would get the feelings not the words. After all, love is incomplete without a little exaggeration isn't it?

I entered my class and saw her sitting alone, maybe waiting for me.

'Hey there!' she said as the moment I entered the class.

'Hi!' I said and smiled, sitting next to her.

'Someone's looking really sexy' she said and I winked.

'Sexy...I don't know why but I hate this word' I said.

'Okay...Someone's looking really ugly' she said and slapped my arm playfully.

I took a quick scan of the class. Her friends were absent and only Dhananjay had arrived till now, only his bag lying on his desk.

'Mohini, I want to say something to you' I said. She looked at me, alert than ever.

'Yes' she said.

'I like you' I whispered as soft as possible. A smile appeared on her face that extended from her right ear to the left. She kind of blushed.

'Are you serious?' she said stuttering.

'Of course stupid I am' I said and grinned. She kept looking at me.

'What? Say something' I said. She still was lost in her thought.

'I...I am confused. No comments' she said and smiled.

No comments? Why was she acting like a minister who was asked a question about a scam?

'Its okay' I said and took out the wrapped chocolate out of my bag.

'What's this?' she said, still blushing.

'It's a gift. From your best friend. Don't open it now. Open it when you are home' I said and she again smiled.

'You are an idiot' she said playfully.

'Idiot in love' I wanted to say but smile instead.

We behaved like we used to that day. We laughed, smiled and it felt like I had never told her that I liked her. Maybe she knew it from the beginning. Maybe she doesn't wants to hurt me.

Everything went down with me except that 'no comments' thing. Has she realised that she deserved a better boy than me? Has she fell in love with that rich hot shot? Am I disturbing their love story? The questions were roaming in my brain as butterflies flew in my stomach.

What will she say to me after reading that note?

Will she slap me?

What if she ends our friendship?

What if things get worse? Like she gets that rich hotshot to beat me up?

Exhausted, tired and confused, I sat on my bed after coming back home from tuition. There was a text from her. I prayed to every god I knew for it to be a happy news. I opened the text.

"Awww. That's really very very very sweet of you! There was no need of chocolate! I will become fat! That note is really sweet. Thank you Sharief!!!!!" She had texted. Going from the level of exclamatory marks in the sentences, it was surely a successful mission.

"Your welcome love" I texted with a heart.

"Good night" she texted me with a blushing smile. I put the phone aside and widely smiled looking at the roof.

My phone bleeped. A notification from Facebook.

"Mohini Sharma updated her status 'Sometimes even little things can make you fall!' "

I smiled. *Yes!!!!!!*

IV

Mohini Sharma

What should I tell him? That I don't like him anymore? That he is nothing but a friend for me now?

Those were the old days when I used to like him. Its only after the 13th year, we the females realise their true value!

I admit that I hid the fact that I liked Umaan more now. He's hot, he's sexy, he's everything Sharief can never be.

Still, Sharief is a guy with the golden heart. His attempts in making me smile and laugh...I can never forget them!

Umaan promises me a good life. A life that is full of fun, pleasure, thrill and shopping!

On the other hand, Sharief has something that I think is way more precious than something Umaan can ever afford. I am talking about love.

I don't know why but I have gut feeling that Sharief will never cheat. He's literally the guy with the golden heart. He'll try to work hard for making the relation work.

I am confused. Like seriously. I am not saying that Sharief's ugly or something. He's still the cutest guy I have ever met. Yet, this decision of mine affects three lives.

My phone bleeped. I opened it. It was from an unknown number.

"I am sorry" the message said. I scratched my head and lied back on the bed.

Who needs to apologize to me? Why does someone wants to apologize to me?

I ignored the message and kept the phone aside.

Should I tell Umaan? About Sharief?

What if he loses his cool and then beats the living shit out of him?

I shifted in the bed as disturbing images appeared in my head. I shook my head.

The phone again bleeped. I opened it. It was the same number again.

"I said I am sorry Mohini" the message read.

Okay, now that's enough.

"Who the hell are you? Who gave me your number? Why are you texting me?" I typed furiously and sent.

At that very moment, my phone started to ring. It was the same number that was disturbing me till now. After five seconds, I picked it up.

'Mohini' the voice said from the other side.

'Yes' I said trying to be as calm as possible. The sound was crackling due to network disturbances but I had heard that voice before.

'You forgot me?' The voice said. The voice was recognised at that very instant by my brain. It was Diveesh.

'Who gave me your number! I am hanging up!' I snapped at him.

He lived just two streets next to my house. We were good friends. I visited his house quite often and he visited mine. It had been three months since that Slap incident had happened. I had cut all sort of contacts with him after that. Still, here he is calling me on my phone after three months to apologize? How's this possible?

'I am sorry Mohini. I…Sharief was right…I am sorry…I said shit about you' he said.

'Its okay' I said after a ten second pause. He was my good friend. Everyone deserves a second chance.

'Thank you so much Mohini…Thank you so very much!' He said.

'Hmm' I said.

'Can you open the door please?' He said.

Shit! He's here!

'Wait a second' I said and hung up. I picked up the clothes from the bed and stuffed them in the closet and ran downstairs.

'Maa. Diveesh's here' I shouted.

She looked at me in surprise. They have been asking me about Diveesh since the past three months. He kept calling, kept visiting our home and I kept ignoring.

I opened the door and there he was. The short guy dressed in a blue T-shirt and brown pants holding a big chocolate in his hand.

'After all this time…' he said.

'Always' I said and tears fell from his face.

Yes! That bastard was regretting what he had done!

He entered the home and greeted Maa. She blessed him and we came upstairs, in my room.

'This feels like a long time. I know you have stuffed those clothes in there' he said pointing towards the closet. He was a bastard. He knew everything.

'Shut up' I said and he laughed.

'I hope you have accepted my sincere apology. These rumours had made me sick. I couldn't believe that you can do something like that. It was shit. A mental torture' he said more sobbed.

'Hey…Forget about it' I said and fired the play station to power, 'Still know how to play?'

'How to play? Still know how to kick your ass' he said and picked up the controller.

We played Tekken for the next half an hour. Like always, he had beaten me up. He played good, no doubt at it.

What Diveesh and I shared was far far different from what Sharief and I shared. In Diveesh's case, we talked a lot but in Sharief's case even if we talked less, we communicated more.

'How's Umaan?' he asked with sweat beads appearing on his face. He dances a lot while playing.

'He's fine' I said, my mind still hovering between Sharief and Umaan. It has been two weeks since he told me he loves me. I still haven't given any answer to him

'Hey…can I ask you something?' I said. It was time to end this confusing nonsense now!

'Yes' he said.

'What does Sharief thinks of me?' I spoke as soft as possible and smiled. I wanted to know if he was seriously in love with me or was just trying to cheer me up. Both of them were in the same class since sixth and he must be knowing every bit of Sharief's mind!

'Like? I see where this is going!' he said and laughed. I smacked his head softly.

'Tell me…' I said as he cut me in mid sentence.

'He fantasises about you' he said with serious expressions. All the reactions in my brain stopped and my face turned pale.

Seriously? He is that kind of boy?

'No…This isn't possible. He isn't that kind of boy!' I said, throwing my hand in air.

'He is…He told me he wants to fuck your brains out. He is a fucking pervert. He keeps touching you intentionally and you don't even notice! Fuck!' he shouted.

'You are lying' I said.

'He told me that you are so fucking sexy and hot, why do you only keep the profile picture of your face and not of your perfect boobs and that ass! He was literally shagging while saying this! Fucking son of a bitch, he's a hypocrite. Wants to have sex with you, nothing more!' he said looking down.

A tear rolled down my cheek. I have never been so much humiliated before. How can he? This isn't possible! He must be lying.

But on the other hand, he was kind of right. He kept messaging me that I looked beautiful…Was he only attracted to my body?

'Hey, cheer up' he said.

Cheer up? The guy who makes me feel so special everyday wants to fuck my brains out? He's a hypocrite! A god damn hypocrite! Losers like him never get a girl! He doesn't deserves me! Even as a friend! He lied to me.

'Can you please leave now' I sobbed.

'Okay, I am going. But remember, I am always there for you' he said and stood up to leave. I heard the sound of the door closing. I sat on the bed motionless, like a trauma had hit me hard. I had no faith in humanity and innocence now, even if it meant turning cold and bitter for him.

A text came from Sharief. I opened it.

"Hey darling! How's life" the message read. I never wanted to contact him again now. He had stabbed in my back.

"I am not your darling! Life? He's fine" I texted him. That asshole deserved to be burnt with jealousy.

"Good night" he texted. I deleted all our previous chats and blocked him on Whatsapp as well as Instagram. He no longer was a part of the world. At least, for me.

Sharief Malhotra

It has been two months since she has talked with me. She even got her seat shifted away from me. I should have never told her that I loved her. Deep down, I knew it would destroy our friendship.

She didn't even bothered to text me back. My shayaries now received only those two blue ticks now. She must have been following the 'Law of conservation of time' that says "If a person is giving you less time, they are surely giving someone else more!".

I knew who the other guy was. Umaan, the rich hotshot or should I put like this, the rich hot shit.

She had blocked me on Whatsapp and on Instagram. The last thing she did before blocking me on Instagram was write 'Karma is a bitch boy' on my last post. *Why the fuck was I seeing this? Why is Karma a bitch for me? Just because I love her and told her this, does that means that I did wrong?*

We didn't talk much now. To be honest, we didn't talked at all.

There was something that was keeping me from believing that it was because I told her that I loved her. We were talking like we always did even two weeks after that day. But suddenly, only god knows what had happened.

"Why are you not talking to me?" I texted her. Thank god she had blocked me now, the messages were now being received by her but still, I couldn't see her profile picture. She must have deleted my number!

"Don't you have anyone else to talk to?" she texted. Her reply was rude. I frowned.

"I have a million people to talk to but still…they don't give me the happiness I get talking to you" I texted.

"Oh please. I don't like to talk to you. Now you know that, stop texting me. Go to hell!" her text ripped my heart apart.

I didn't further reply to her. It felt like a huge chainsaw just passed right through my chest.

The girl I loved more than my life, the girl I never wanted to lose, my best friend was now not talking with me. It hurts.

I felt a need to confront her. Yes, I needed to confront her. How could she destroy my perfectly happy life?

It must have been because of that rich motherfucker. Well, my sources revealed he was not rich. Just upper middle class shit guy trying to feel rich and top of the world. I wanted to slap him, kill him with a hammer and bury him in the trunk of my car. If he was the one who took my best friend away from me, he would have to pay for it.

I turned myself into a depressed idiot. I won't call it depression. Depression is when your girlfriend dumps you. It was something funnier. I don't think you can call it a 'Break up' when your crush dumps you!

Everyday I attempted to confront her but failed miserably. She won't talk to me, will try to avoid me when with her friends, walked fast when she saw me. She literally was using all means of torture on my little heart.

I know that she is beautiful and I am ugly as fuck! We don't match. Yes, we never did. It was just by coincidence that she became friends with me. It was a coincidence we became best friends. It was a coincidence that I fell in love with her. Coincidences are sometimes bitch!

I kept thinking about her. All the time. I recalled our past happy days. Those past stale chapatti and pickle dates. I had turned into a cry baby though I didn't shed much tears but wanted to. My emotions were sinking in an ocean.

Things turned worst in tenth standard. First, I joined the same coaching centre as hers. Though I got a separate batch, I still took came early just to see her lovely face.

One some days, Umaan would drop her there. They would pass flying kisses to each other. She noticed me from the corner of her eyes but ignored me and kept walking swiftly into the institute.

The moment she entered the institute and Umaan ignited his car again, I prayed to god that may he get caught in some deadly accident and end up losing a limb or something. I didn't wanted god to kill him. I didn't wanted god to kill anyone.

The only thing that kept me from turning into a drunkard and a sociopath was studies. I studied my ass off. All the free periods in the school, all the games periods, the weekends, the family functions, the birthday parties; I skipped them all.

I failed miserably at many subjects. Mathematics just raped me. I was on the verge of flunking. Maybe the amount or the time you study can never do anything unless there's a spark of joy inside you. For now, my spark of joy was ignoring me like hell and I hated it.

For her, I didn't even exist now. She looked right through me. Sometimes, will I stood alone in the school corridors, she just walked past me like I was a complete stranger. Like we had never met before. I mentally kicked my mind every second of my life for telling her that I liked her.

The year passed. A lot of ignoring and hard works later, the result was out. CBSE had screwed some happy lives once again.

'How is this even possible? You used to be on your laptop all day, studying hard. How can this be so?' my neighbour said as he scrolled down my result on the official website. It showed 'CGPA 8.8'. Yes, you read it right, my neighbour. Indian neighbours love interfering in their neighbour's life. Be it some relation, results, some night out, a neighbour is always there for you to question you!.

‘Don’t you know something like ‘Porn hub’ exists?’ I murmured.

‘What?’ he said as he didn’t hear it.

‘Nothing. It’s okay. 8.8 is cool I guess’ I lied. The wifi in our home was down (because I had unbolted some screws in the router circuit because I knew that I had fucked up with my result), that’s why I was here in his home. 8.8 is like the end of this world for me. The moment I’ll tell my parents, who had pushed me out as soon as they heard the news of the result, they’ll surely kick my ass and throw me out of home. You know, just like in the movies.

‘Can I check another result?’ I said as he raised his eyebrow.

‘Tell me the roll number’ He said as I narrated him with Mohini’s roll number and date of birth. As soon as the result loaded, a funny sound came out of nowhere. Maybe it was the sound of his balls in his mouth!

’T…Te…Ten’ he announced as I smiled. Yes, the intelligent feminist had got perfect ten.

This gave me another reason to think why we never were perfect for each other. At least I wasn’t for her. I was thankful to CBSE for the eye opener. 8.8 and 10 were way too far from each other. She was a topper, I was an under achiever that’s all.

With a smile on my face, I left his home and entered mine. The situation resembled same as that outside of an operation theatre where a delivery was being held. My father sat on the sofa staring at his phone cursing the hell out to BSNL for their useless wifi router and my mother talking to a relative on her phone.

‘8.8’ I said smiling. I wasn’t smiling for myself. I was smiling for Mohini. I was happy for her.

‘What?’ both of them said in unison and their expression turned like the doctor had just announced “Sorry but either we can save the child or the mother”. One could literally hear a pooja thali dropping in the background.

My CGPA didn't mattered for me as much as Mohini's did. She got her photo in the newspaper and I had collected a cut out of it. Not only that, our coaching had also given an advertisement that had her photo too. I had collected maybe hundreds of those pamphlets and stuffed them under my bed.

It wasn't as bad as expected for me. The best thing was that other kids of my age in our clan didn't even managed to touch the mark of '8' let alone 'eight fucking point eight'. God helped me with it. Their mothers may be suing god soon on the product they got delivered with when they payed in terms of 'fasts'.

A few days later, when I was on my laptop, searching for career options in medical field I received a call. It was from Guntas, one of my best friends also called as the bone breaker of the class.

'Celebrations!!' he shouted doing heavy damage to my internal ear.

'Yes! It calls for celebrations!' I said.

'Movie?' he said.

'Which one?'

'NH 10. Let's go bro! You, me, momos, Dhananjay and Mohini' he said as a wide smile appeared on my face the moment I heard her name.

To some of you trying to figure out who is 'Momos', Divyam, one of the members of our squad had got the nick name of momos because of his habit at gulping down numerous dumplings down at once!

'Yeah. Sure. Tomorrow?' I said looking at the calendar. It was a Saturday tomorrow.

'Will you get the tickets? We'll pay you later' he said as I let out a laugh.

'I will surely get them. And dare to pay me, consider it as a treat!' I said as he hung up.

I finally had a chance to confront Mohini.

V

I dressed in a fine blue shirt with dark denim jeans. Adjusted my hair in the mirror and applied the new perfume I had just bought. I looked fine. Better than my normal appearance.

I was ready to confront her today. After all this time, it was today that had given me the perfect moment to make things clear between us. I never pushed her for a relationship but neither had I wanted our friendship to end. I missed our friendship.

I sat in the car. The driver smiled at me.

Its now or never!

'Where to sir?' he asked looking at me.

'Movie time cinemas' I said as he drove off in thin air.

Fifteen minutes later, I was there. The ticket counters were empty as hell. The opening of Wave Cinemas in the city had done quite some damage to this theatre. It god better picture quality and new seats. Still, this one was in business because many couples (hardly eighteen or nineteen) came here. It was a parents proof place though I still bumped into my friend's father when I was here to watch Jism 2!

'Five tickets for the NH 10' I said as the half sleepy guy who was watching porn till now minimised that window and printed five tickets for me.

I handed him the money and sat aside. The sun was burning. It was June and the world cup was rocking the hearts. I fished out my phone and started watching Australia vs Afghanistan match.

Half an hour later, I felt a pat at my back and saw Dhananjay standing there. I hugged him tightly. He wasn't friend for me. He was family.

'Where are the other guys?' I said. He took out his phone and called Guntas on loud speaker.

'Coming! There's so much fucking traffic! Oh god!' he gasped and hung up. Both of us made face and he sat next to me. It must be a funny sight watching two guys sitting on a thin platform in a theatre's parking.

'So how's life?' he said and smiled.

'It's good' I said.

'Its? Until yesterday, it was 'she's good' and now suddenly 'It's good'? Why?' he asked with a serious expression.

'It's a long story' I said. For the first time I had hidden something for so long.

'So what? Tell me' he said.

'She's ignoring…' I had just started as I heard a horn. They were here. The car came to a halt and she stepped out. She looked extra fine with blue eye liner applied perfectly, her blue eyes shining in broad daylight!

'*Isko kyu bulaya?'* She muttered the moment she saw me. Though she had said it in the softest tone possible, still being a pervert, I was staring at her lips and lip read her.

Okay, so here is a guy who buys the tickets for you and is waiting for maybe since the last one hour for you to come. And instead of thank you or any greetings, you say 'Why did you called him?'. Isn't it rude? Isn't it unfair?

Anger burnt in my eyes. The sun no longer had any effect on me. I was burning from inside. You can take the bullet once but not twice!

I waved at Guntas and Divyam and hugged them. My eyes ignored all sort of contact with hers. I didn't wanted to be a part of their stupid movie plan anymore. I wanted to borrow a lighter from the guy standing next to me and burn those tickets in front of her. Not only those tickets, had I wanted to burn her completely down!

'Let's go inside' she said as I handed her the tickets without even looking at her. It was clear from my face that I was angry as fuck. I had clenched my fists tight.

'Popcorn?' she said looking at me. I ignored her and entered the hall. She sat three seats away from me, with a tub of popcorn and a small coke in her hand.

The movie started. It was based on 'Honour killing'. Though it was an 'A' certified movie, we were still inside the hall, watching the movie and enjoying every bit of it.

'Why the fuck are you tickling my feet?' Dhananjay said.

'I am not' I said, already annoyed.

'Shut up. See. You again are. Fuck you' he whispered slowly.

'Wait' I said and turned the flash light of the phone on towards the leg space of the seats. To our horror, there were 'rats'!

'Fuck!' We both shouted and stood in unison. The others in the theatre looked at us awkwardly.

'Sorry' I said in air and sat on the seat that were two rows forward. Dhananjay followed me too.

The movie featured Anushka Sharma. Well, I used to call Mohini Anushka because both of them had the same face cut. I was no more interested in either watching Anushka or Mohini but just for the sake of the money I just blew up, I kept glued to my seat for two and a half hour.

The halogens were up as the movie ended. All of us stood up.

'Pizza' Guntas said, rubbing his stomach.

'Sure. Lets go' Divyam said as we exited the hall.

We entered 'Pizza Hut' and sat on a round table with Mohini sitting in front of me. She kept staring at me, looking into my eyes, examining my angry as fuck expressions!

'Order whatever you people want to. I have some important work. Got to leave' I lied as I fished out my phone. I no longer wanted to sit here, in front of the girl who fucked my happiness.

'Just keep sitting' They said in unison. I stood up from the table and left.

Dhananjay pulled me by my hand but still I managed to get myself free from his grip. The rest of them looked at me in horror.

I went to the Dominos and ordered a small pizza for my sister. She had said that she wanted to have one and being a good brother, I had to buy one for her.

'What's the problem bhai?' Dhananjay said as I fished out my wallet and paid for the bill.

'I don't want to be a part of this party anymore. You understand? ANYMORE!' I shouted as every head turned to us.

I had shouted at him for the first time in these eight years since we were friends. A tear rolled down my cheek.

'Let's go outside. I want to talk' I barely managed to say and dragged him outside. We sat in the stairs that lead to the first floor.

'She said "Issey kyu bulaya" Like what the fuck?' I said and cried. His expressions were confused as ever.

'What happened?' He said, 'who said this?'

'Mohini' I said and sobbed.

'I have seen that since last year, both of you haven't been quite nice to each other. Well to be precise, she hasn't been nice to you. She ignored you for so many time and here you are, sulking and sobbing. What's the matter dude? Why don't you tell me the whole story?' He said. I looked at his face. He was concerned for me. Indeed, he was.

I narrated him the whole story of how I told her that I loved her, how she ignored me like hell and how much fucked up I felt.

'So you never confronted her?' He said, patting my back.

'Never got the chance to' I said.

'You should talk to her. What's keeping her away from you. You should sort it out' He said. Divyam was looking for us and gave a confused expression the moment he saw us.

'What the hell are you guys doing here? It has been fifteen minutes since you have been missing' he said.

'Sorry guys but I disturbed your perfect plan. I shouldn't have' I said and folded my hands.

'What's wrong with you Sharief?' He said. I shook my head as Dhananjay suddenly started to walk towards the pizza hut again.

'Where are you going?' I shouted from behind. He didn't reply me. He was surely going to her.

I hugged Divyam and faked another call to make him realise that I was damn busy. Collecting the pizza for my sister from Dominos as Dhananjay came running towards me.

'She's ashamed' he said. The expression on my face became pale.

'Ashamed? Of what?' I said.

'Of what she did with you' he said.

'What did you tell her?'

'Nothing. Just made her realise she did wrong' he said.

I entered the pizza hut again and saw Mohini's face pale yellow. She was on her phone doing something. I placed a five hundred bucks note on the table.

'I am sorry guys. I won't have food but here's my contribution' I announced as everyone raised their eyebrows.

Mohini was still on her phone, doing something. God knows what she was doing.

'This isn't fair' Guntas and Divyam said in unison.

'Everything is fair in love and war' I said as Mohini looked at me, expressionless and ashamed.

'Bye' I said as I left them. I hugged Dhananjay as I sat in the car.

The driver had seen that I was in a bad mood.

'What happened sir?' He said.

'Nothing. Hurry up please' I said as I opened my whatsapp and changed my status to "That moment when someone lip reads you saying *"Isko kyu bulaya"*.

Suddenly my phone pinged. It was a message from Mohini.

"Why did you left so early? :/" the text read. I saw it and ignored it.

Another text.

"What's it with your status?"

I clutched my phone hard. So hard, that the tempered glass cracked. I was angry as fuck.

My phone rang. It was a call from Guntas.

'I know why you left. And I have something to tell to you' he said.

'Where are you?' I said.

'Leave it. It's Diveesh. Mohini had called me last night when I called her to invite her to the party and said, "Diveesh said Sharief fantasise about me. He says Why do I only keep the profile picture of my face and not my body? He also said that I am sexy as fuck and he wants to fuck my brains out" She was hurt and said that she feels insecure with you. Don't tell anyone this but she had told me not to invite you' he whispered slowly.

'What?' I said coming back to senses.

Diveesh? That motherfucking son of a bitch!

'Leave it. Just don't tell anyone whatever I had told you. Bye' he said and hung up.

I punched the window imagining it as his face and it shattered into pieces. He had to pay. That son of a bitch. Motherfucker.

It hurts when people trust five minutes long chat over a five years long friendship!

Three Months Later

The past three months had changed a lot in me and my life too. I had forgiven Diveesh. Yes, I had forgiven him.

His father had died; his family was kind of going through tough times. I didn't want to worsen their condition. It's okay if he betrayed me, everyone deserves a second chance.

On the other hand, my feelings for Mohini kept on growing day by day.

She said she was okay with me and that she realised that Diveesh had lied. But this mood of hers was only short lived and again, she was in her usual ignoring mode.

I don't know why I loved her. Maybe I was a good guy. Maybe I was being too generous to her. She had perfectly screwed me but I still was attempting in making her happy. After all, it wasn't her mistake. It was Diveesh's for that son of a bitch lied to her. She simply believed a rumour.

'You know Mohini is an angel' I said to Utsav while wiping my dirty glasses with a cloth. We sat in the NesCafe as it was our usual recess time in tuition. He sipped a little from his *aukaat-ke-andar-waali coffee.* I smiled at him as I imagined her perfect face.

'Yes. Mankind's angel!' He said and chuckled. I made a face

"Don't you have someone else to talk!" She doesn't deserve the love you are giving it to her!' He said mimicking her voice. I glared at that bastard.

'Fuck you. That is a thing of past. She is beautiful; so much beautiful that you can't imagine' I said slapping playfully at that assholes face, 'much beautiful from S.W.A.T!'

'Bitch please!' He said a little hurt as I spoke the truth. My crush is surely beautiful than his's.

You just can't compare Freedom 251 and iPhone 6s

'Hey it's her birthday. What do you think I should gift her?' I asked a little worried. 14th September was the date when an angel was born. Angel named Mohini with blue eyes!

'Gift her some novel. Maybe...Half girlfriend!' He said after a pause. Maybe the novel would do the thing.

'Three days are left Mr Malhotra' he said breaking my chain of thoughts 'better do it fast.'

My phone rang. It was the remainder that the break has ended. I gestured him and we left the cafe.

I acted like I was going to charge at him, mimicking the lift scene from 'Fifty Shades of Grey'. We both laughed at the end.

'No buddy. Only one girl is there in my life. Mohini' I said as we exited the elevator and entered the class.

I spent the next one and a half hour studying biology.

'Hello? Utsav there?' I said as someone picked on his landline. A broken voice.

'Yes. Sharief' he said, 'why the fuck are you calling so late at my landline?'

'Do you think a novel will be good?' I asked as my mind was confused between novels, chocolates, flowers, cards and many more.

'Fuck you! Fuck you man. At eleven o'clock there is a guy calling me to discuss what he should gift his crush on her birthday? Are you insane?' He said in a tired tone.

'Insane…in love' I said and he laughed.

'Yes, the novel will do it. Now please let me sleep' he said in a tone my grandfather speaks when I ask him for money.

'Okay. Bye' I said and smiled widely like an idiot. *Yes, I love her. She is only mine. Even though I know she doesn't seem interested in me, yet I feel like it's my responsibility to make her feel special.*

'Hahaha' Akshit laughed as I told him my plans to gift a novel to Mohini on her birthday, 'seriously? A novel? You know what, its people like you who go to Shirdi on a bachelor party' He laughed hard again. 'You don't understand love. It is deep. Gift her something she will remember forever. Something that stays with her. Not something that she ends up selling to a rag picker!' His words were like bullet shots right through my heart.

'Bro I told you. I got no experience' I said and made a face. We were in the school. My squad wanted to know what my plans were for her birthday. The only one that laughed out of them was Akshit.

'As if I got experience. It's like asking a chain smoker that *"Bhaiya yeh nicotine free chewing gum kahaan milenge"* he said and burst into laughter again. Thankfully Priyanshu slapped his face as his jokes become far from intolerable.

See. People like Akshit with a fucked up sense of humour are the one that force Aamir Khan to say 'India is intolerant.'

'Sharief do whatever your heart says. He will keep speaking shit' Priyanshu said as Aryaman hugged him and Akshit brought his middle finger close to his face.

'I will gift her novel' I said as at that very instant, the teacher arrived in our class and we; like everyday acted as if we were studying.

• • • 13th September • • •

I examined the blue gift wrap carefully. Mr Aryaman Dubey had done its job. I had given him the novel I bought to gift wrap and he had accomplished his task.

'Love you Dubey' I said; touching the pink ribbon on it. It looked beautiful but not more than Mohini.

All the other members of my group whistled. Their whistle reminded me of one of the theatres in Bihar I had visited once. Mohini entered the class. She looked at me and I smiled. She smiled back and sat on her seat. It was my plan to ignore her and don't even let her know that I knew of her birthday. She would be surprised. It was in sixth period; the physical ed. period when the whole class was empty other than my group of six friends. It was when I decided to take my plan forward.

I took the wrapped novel and sneaked it in Mohini's bag. I put it in such a way so that she wouldn't notice it.

You need balls to open a girl's bag without her permission honey!

In half an hour she returned to class with her group of friends. We were friends since sixth grade and I knew her well. So well that I already predicted that she won't touch her bag until the school gets over. She was lazy.

I was right. She didn't touch her bag until the bell rang, she just picked it and started to walk. I exchanged hugs with my friends and my heart did cartwheels inside. *Tomorrow, I am going to let her know. That I love her...*

* * *

I slapped myself to keep myself awake till midnight. 'Operation call' was also one of my plans. I would call her at midnight to congratulate her and to tell her that I love her. I checked the clock, it was 11:59. I picked up my phone and dialled her number.

She picked up after two rings.

'Hello' her sweet voice vanished all the sleepiness I had. My heart ran fast.

You know while talking to your crush, your heart runs faster than Usain Bolt!

'H…Hel…Hello Mohini. Sharief here' I said stammering.

'Who?' She said. *She must have deleted my phone number!*

'What the fuck?' She said, words I never thought existed in her.

'Happy birthday!' I said in a sweet tone.

'Who the fuck on earth gave you the permission to slide that fucking novel in my bag without telling me? What the fuck do you think you are huh? Shah rukh khan?' She said as tears emerged in my eyes. Of course she didn't like me. But she didn't had the moral rights to insult my feelings.

'I thought you would like it!' I said, crying.

'Fuck your imagination. You even think that I like you don't you?' She glared, 'Thanks by the way' she hung up.

I threw the fucking phone on the bed and cried. I let the tears flow out. I let myself look like a mother fucker. I cried and cried, endlessly.

Who the fuck does she thinks she is?

She ain't that beautiful!

She took the advantage of your gentle and good behaviour! She fucked you Mr Malhotra

Voices rang inside my head hurting me. Her words repeated like 80's songs do on All India Radio.

I was fucked up

I picked my phone and called Utsav. I checked the time, it was 12:30.

After two tries and on fifth ring he picked up.

'Who the fuck is there?' He said in a usually tired tone. 'Hey buddy its me. Wassup?' I said still crying but trying to hide my sadness behind fake enthusiasm.

'If you are again going to talk about the gift, FUCK YOU!' He said.

'Just wanted to let you know. I don't love Mohini anymore' I said and I imagine him getting struck with a 1200 Volt current at that very instant.

You know the worst thing about human heart? Once the feelings for someone start, they just keep growing. But once they end, they just fucking end…

VI

I didn't slept that night. Clock seemed to run faster. *What does she thinks of herself?*

'You see Sharief, it's the good people that get broken in the end!' *My optimistic side said; 'your only mistake is being good and believe me, whatever you are doing is right'.*

'It's not your mistake! It's a choice you made foolish! You could have abused her right on that phone! Why did you wasted those Two Fifty bucks!' My idiotic side said.

'You never abused a girl. Then why will you? You don't bite back a dog when it bites you! Just remember who you are, Mr. Malhotra.'

'Don't listen to him! He sucks anyway' the idiot inside me shouted as I heard some sounds of a brawl. Maybe it was the optimist and the idiot inside me, fighting.

I looked at the clock. It was 6:00 of the morning. It was the time of sun rise. I got off my bed and wore my shoes.

I got out of my home to catch some fresh air. I couldn't bear those two idiots fighting anymore. The streets were scarcely filled with Municipality workers standing with brooms doing their job of cleaning. After twenty five minutes of jogging, I stopped and sat aside on the footpath.

I saw a dog; a street dog to be particular. It ran from one worker to another, in search of food. Some of them gave it, some didn't. Yet the dog didn't stop. What mattered for it was 'food' not 'the one offering it'. I imagined myself in place of the dog.

The only difference was that it was 'Love' in my case that I was hungry of.

Maybe it was the right time to move on.

Of course, you cannot live on fake hopes for the rest of the time.

Tears again appeared in my eyes. I had done enough of crying last night and did not wanted to do that anymore. I rubbed my eyes and stood up, walking towards my home again.

'Good morning Sharief' I heard my dad say as I just entered the home. He was sitting on the sofa in the living room, holding the morning's newspaper and examining it like a jeweller examines a jewel.

We Indians are very fond of eating, discussing people and sometimes newspapers too!

'Morning dad' I said in a sad tone, unusual of me.

'All okay?' He said as he sensed my mood.

'Yes yes' I said as I went to the washroom for a shower and got ready for the school afterwards.

I entered the class like I did always. The only difference is that my always smiling face looked sad and depressed. My friends started asking me details on 'Operation Mid Night Call'. Utsav was also there. He knew everything but still kept quite. I didn't respond to anyone.

'Mohini got struck in your love or not' Aryaman said. He was the shortest in our group. I and Aryaman were extreme cases. He was short, with no beard or even moustache looking like Puberty just skipped him like a red light by an auto driver. On the other hand, I was the taller, bulkier and bearded one.

'He doesn't wants to talk about that right now. Leave him alone doobs' Utsav said looking at my face.

'Say something. Say something brother' Akshit said. I looked at him and tears started to flow at unstoppable pace from my eyes. He came near me and hugged me tightly.

'Tell me the whole thing. Nobody makes my brother cry!' He said as all the other seven boys of our group also leaped forward to hug me. I collected myself and narrated the whole incident of last night to them.

'Bitch she is!' Priyanshu said as everyone nodded along.

'Don't abuse her please!' I said as his words hurt me.

'See, even though being hurt so much by her you couldn't bear anyone abusing her' a voice said from inside.

'Sharief I had told you earlier too. This girl doesn't deserves what you are giving her' Utsav spoke, holding my hand firmly.

'You need to confront her! Yes, you need to' Akshit said standing up from his desk. I knew where he was going. To Mohini.

I saw her standing outside, in the corridor. This is what we usually do when the teacher hasn't arrived. I grabbed his hand to stop him. Unfortunately, I was a little late.

'Who the hell gave you the permission to hurt my brother huh? You hypocrite bitch!' Akshit said as Mohini's friends looked at her in horror.

'This is what he deserves. Look at his face! He will be my boyfriend? My foot!' She said, looking straight into Akshit's eyes. Their *kind-of-stare-game* gave me enough time to look at Mohini's blue, irresistible eyes.

'You will die in hell! You hurt such a good person, you will realise this later!' He said again, eyes fixed at her face.

'Good person? Ask him what he spoke about me to Diveesh and then come to me' she said, walking away from us in the class.

'What did you told Diveesh about Mohini?' Akshit said holding both of my shoulders. He looked extra tensed and angry.

'Can you believe that I can say "Mohini is a slut. Why doesn't she wear short clothes, she got such a sexy body"?' I said as my heart started beating fast, clenching my fists.

'Are you serious? That short cheap liar bastard!' He said punching the wall. I never abused a girl in my life and I never will.

'You look a little down. What happened?' He said as we entered the class again. I saw her again and sat on my seat.

'Nothing. Just a little depressed about yesterday' I said cracking my knuckles.

'You know there are some people which we need and some which we deserve. She might be the one which you need; but not the one you deserve. You will get the best girl in the world!' He said sipping water from his bottle. I saw at my other friends. Most of them were busy staring their crushes. I opened my notebook and started studying; ignoring the girl that screwed me for the rest of the time.

I had turned myself into one of those people you see in depressed movies. I tried doing what my friends said, that according to them "will surely help me get over her".

Their ideas were mainly watching HD porn, going out with random girls, staring at girls like I am going to swallow them raw. Though their ideas sucked as bad as their sense of humour, the first one helped me a little. It just raised my monthly expenses on tissue papers.

I changed my image completely in front of my teachers and my family. Now, I was the same old guy which I used to be before stepping into the heaven called '6th C'.

I studied hard and didn't care if my spark of joy still existed or not.

I literally had no more interest in girls now. In the past few weeks, I had dated maybe ten to fifteen girls and trust me, it had ended really badly.

Either I had failed attempted to kiss them and they slapped me or I ended up telling fake stories about my past. Some of them were like "I am gay, like seriously. I was sexually abused at the age of twelve", some "I am a sadist". On a scale of five, I literally rate my creativity minus five!

I don't even remember their names. I admit that most of them seemed keenly interested in me. For me, it was nothing but an attempt to move on from the pain that has caused by these last fucking five years!

'Coffee?' Smriti, another random date that my friends had arranged asked me as we sat in the Cafe Coffee Day.

'Devil's own' I said as she smiled. She was different from all the girls I had dated till now. Her cheeks were pinkish and a little chubby and she was in a really fit shape.

'So tell me about yourself' she said as she ordered two devil's own and a brownie.

'I am a nerd. That's all' I said as she raised an eyebrow.

'That's really the perfect example of 'underestimating' yourself' she said. She was a commerce student, my friends had told me and studied in KC.

'You tell me something about yourself' I said as I fished out my phone and started reading news articles.

'I am a nerd too' she said and laughed.

Was it a joke?

'My friends told me that you have gone through a heart break. It must have been worse' she said with concern shining in all parts of her eye.

'Heart break...um...I don't know if you can call it a heart break or not' I said rubbing my chin. The waiter arrived with the coffee.

'Tell me. Whatever happened. I am good at solving problems but sometimes...It's me who becomes the problem' she said and winked. She picked her coffee up and started sipping it. Her lips were covered with little traces of the whipped cream. It was damn...such a pervert I am!

I told her everything about me and Mohini in the next fifteen minutes. She listened to me with the expressions same as I had, in childhood, when my grandma used to tell me a story.

'That's really absurd' she said, still sipping from the empty glass with her straw, making noises.

'What's absurd? What I did?' I said.

'No...no. What she did. She could have just asked you if you had said those things or not. What did she do? Cut off all contacts with you, like you don't even exist and make you feel guilty for something you never did! Give me her number' she said. I shook my head.

She was quite right according to me. If I were on Mohini's side, I would have called my friend and sorted things out. Ignoring never gave anyone anything except some heart breaks, some ego issues and some tissue papers!

'You are right' I said and smiled. This was the first time I had smiled from my heart, not those fake smiles post *Operation Midnight Call.*

'Actually...I have something to tell' she said. I nodded and alerted my ears with full attention.

'I already have a boyfriend. But I think he's double dating me. So only to make him jealous, I came on a date with you' she said. 'I am not sure if he's cheating me or not but from the past few days, he behaves changed' she said as a tear rolled down her cheek.

I passed her a tissue.

'Just go and ask him. Don't just suppose things. Lack of communication can cause serious damage to your love life!' I said.

I thanked god for she already had a boyfriend and I didn't needed my old cheap attempts to end up dates badly, deliberately.

Days passed and I kept myself busy with books and occasionally, with porn sites. Things were really bad for me. Either it was Cos and Sin or Johnny Sin!

'You...look...fucked up' Utsav said as I sat next to him in our tuition, 'Boy when I see your face, I feel that the phrase "Finding love was never easy" is fucking true!'

'Shut up' I said.

'Look around man. So many girls and not even single that you like!' he snapped.

'I don't give a damn Utsav. I have much important things to do with my life rather than sitting in coffee shops and having over priced coffees' I said.

The teacher entered. Piyush sir, our physics teacher. He raised an eyebrow the moment he saw me.

'What's wrong? Why so sad? And this beard?' he asked.

'*Aisey hi sir*' I said.

'I hope everything becomes okay' he said. He probably had assumed that I had a break up.

'Sir may I come in' a never heard before female voice said. The door was just a little open and only her hand was visible.

'New admission?' he said.

'Yes sir' the girl said as the door opened completely.

To be honest, a shiver ran down my spine the moment I saw her.

She was 'PERFECT'. I repeat 'PERFECT'.

'Come in' he said as she came inside and sat on the desk just opposite to me. She high fived Isha. Maybe she was her friend.

I looked at her. Brown complexioned, perfectly in shape (better than Smriti or should I say, better than every girl I have met till now) and a just slightly big conk that added the layer of 'Cuteness' to her face.

She was as tall. My heart beat unusually as I admired her. Beauty was really embedded on every part of her skin.

Her cheeks were baby like. She smiled in a way no one could ever. Her lips, alone, could have won her any beauty pageant. The eyebrows above those big, brownish eyes stole the show.

I kept staring her with my mouth open.

Humans were never so beautiful! She must be an alien. Or a mutant.

By now, I expected her to stand up from her desk and shoot ultra violet rays from her eyes.

Her waist length hairs were perfectly combed. Right now, I felt like an employee of ASI who was examining an extremely beautiful artefact. Her hair flew like someone was standing just behind her, with a table fan in his hands. Those lips made me sweat, even in the air conditioner.

My mouth went dry. My brain planned the possibility of a black out which ends up in me kissing her. Maybe, I was in love with her. See, just five minutes since she entered the class and I am planning my kid's name.

God had put all the Snapchat and B612 filters to shame, at once.

I kept looking at her. I think she noticed. I heard her name being shouted by her friends, 'Mahira'. Damn good name!

The time froze. I could see all the micro particles floating in air. As the teacher asked her questions, her sweet cherry voice made me lose my senses. By now, I gave a damn about how a Pulley worked.

I wanted to talk to her. Maybe we could become friends. After all, from Love to Hatred, everything starts from a 'friendship'.

I picked up my bag and started to move. I ran as slow as possible in order to bump into her and make a conversation. Unfortunately I failed.

She sat in her car and it speed off, leaving smoke and my heart behind!

Every day, I kept looking at her. Maybe I loved her, but I wasn't sure about it.

I trimmed my beard to transform myself from post-interval Varun Dhavan of Badlapur to pre-interval Varun Dhavan. My grades were again normal…I mean low. I started to become happy, just by having a look at her every day. It literally made my day.

'Sharief…' Utsav said patting my back. It was recess time and all of us sat in the class. She was narrating some incident of her school to her friends with a pen swinging in those long, slender and beautiful fingers. How lucky the pen was.

'Wait…' I said, rotating my neck to a suitable angle for the perfect view. I could have been easily mistaken as a Gymnast from a distance.

'I think you like her' he said, raising his eyebrow. She was dressed in a green top with blue jeans.

'I don't' I lied, 'want to be just friends.'

'How can one become just friends on earth when you have nothing to do in your life other than staring her from a distance and eaves dropping on the conversation?'

'Please' I slapped his back. She smiled wide as she ended her narration. Maybe she was talking about her crush. The possibility of this situation made my heart clench.

'Get a side' I said to him, standing from my desk. He was right. We weren't even friends.

He followed my instructions and got a side. I walked slowly towards her desk.

'Mahira' I said. She looked up at me, confused.

'Yes' she said in her honey tone.

'I want to talk to you' I said, 'somewhere private.'

My *Somewhere private* thing brought a lot of 'Oohs' and 'Aahs' in her friends. She nodded and stood up. We went to the last desk of the class and sat.

'Hi' I said in an unusually excited tone, extending my hand towards her.

'Hi' she said, shaking hands with me. I felt so lucky right now, getting to hold those long fingers.

'What do you want to talk about?' she asked. Her voice made my heart beat sound worse than those Generators in Punjabi Weddings, kept for use in case of emergency. My tongue flapped and my brain froze. It felt that I was sitting on an ice berg named 'beauty'.

'Hey' she waved her hand at me, bringing me back to planet earth.

'You are beautiful' I said in reflex. She smiled. Of course, she was beautiful. Most beautiful. Even with a thousand dictionaries thrown towards me at once, I wouldn't be able to find the right word to compliment her beauty.

'Okay, anything else?' she asked.

'Can we be friends?' I asked, with a puppy like glee in my eyes.

'We are already friends; I guess' she said. I mentally jumped from my seat and danced.

The bell rang.

'See you soon, friend' she winked and stood up to leave for her seat.

'Yes' I barely managed to speak.

Days passed and we kept talking endless shit. We did what 'friends' did. Have fun, study together, crack jokes. One such fate full day, my phone bleeped. It was an Instagram notification about a follow request from a username *Mahi_bhatt_mb.* It was her! Mahira Bhatt!

She was as beautiful as ever, even in the pics. I liked and commented on all of them even if that meant I would come across as a desperate guy.

We started texting each other a lot! From a lot I mean a lot! We exchanged our numbers and even continued to text each other after 'Good night'. We became best friends.

Things could only get better!

A few more days after our texting sessions continued, I was confused if I should tell her what I felt for her or not. To be a little sure of my decision, I called Smriti, after few rings she picked up.

'Yes' she said.

'Smriti, is me. Sharief' I said.

'THANK YOU!!! THANK YOU SO VERY MUCH!' she shouted. I rubbed my ear in pain.

'For what?' I asked confused.

'He wasn't cheating on me! NO! HE WASN'T! He was instead planning a surprise birthday party for me!! I love him so very much. Thank you again, Sharief. Else I would have broke up with him now!' she said. I smiled.

'Okay, your welcome. I need a little help of yours' I said.

'Yes' she said.

'There's a girl I like…' I said as she cut me.

'Wohooo!!! At last! Thank god!' she said and chuckled.

'What?' I said as she stopped chuckling.

'Finally! Tell me her name'

'Mahira' I said and blushed. I was acting like an idiot.

'Helluva nice name!' she said. I could sense she was smiling on the other side.

'Should I tell her that I like her?' I asked. The last time I told a girl I liked her, she threw me out of her life.

What if she does the same?

What if she has a boyfriend?

What if I lose her? Even as a friend?

She was again out of my league!

'Tell her you idiot! But not on some text or some note. Tell her face to face! Don't repeat your past mistakes' she said. She was right as always.

'Okay, I am on it. Thank you' I said.

'Thank you again!!' she said as I hung up.

It was Showtime!

Studying in one of the most reputed English medium school of my city, she was one of the friendliest girl I had ever met. The best thing about her was her simplicity. She had passion for dance and art in some part of her heart. I met her just this year and guess what; I fell in love with her.

I smiled at the mirror practicing some greetings in my head. I took my bag as the driver just arrived. It was the time for my tuition.

In half hour I reached my tuition. I took the elevator. I again checked myself in the mirror.

Maybe I found a new example of involuntary actions: A person in love checking him in mirror!

I reached the third floor in thirty seconds. The lift opened and to my surprise, Miss Mahira Bhatt was standing there. On the threshold of our institute.

She wore a red T-shirt and jeans, with her hair set free. The colour of the T-shirt complemented her brown complexion. I was awestruck. I smiled at her, a wide idiotic smirk. I kept staring at her. She looked at me and waved her hand in air.

'Hi' I said, 'Hi Mahira!' With unusually high beating of my heart.

'Hi Sharief!' She said smiling. The smile that melted my heart like ice cream on a hot brownie.

Maybe I can define beautiful now. It's the girl standing right front in me, smiling!

'I want to talk to you' I said, yes I had planned to tell her the truth today. That I loved her. That I not only needed her, I deserved her too.

'Yes' she said, her eyes directly looking into mine.

Miss Mahira Bhatt, I love you...Nah!

Mahira, will you like to come in a relationship with me?...Are you selling some product?

Mahira, I like you...Maybe it can do the magic.

'I like...' I said as suddenly at that particular instant, our chemistry teacher appeared in front of us.

'Students, are you not getting late for your class?' He said adjusting his spectacles.

'Yes sir' we said in unison and started walking towards our class.

The next few hours were the worst of my life. I had to study chemistry and physics, avoid looking too much at Mahira and think of telling her that I loved her.

The bell rang exactly at 7:45. Everybody stood up and started to walk out of the class. Utsav and I walked slowly, my eyes still on Mahira.

'I see your changed behaviour. Stop staring her now! She will know that you are interested in her!' Utsav said slapping my elbow.

She stopped in midway and turned back towards me.

'You wanted to tell me something? Something you like?' She said. Utsav's eyes popped and I signalled him to leave.

'Yes. Maybe we can walk and talk' I said as we started to walk down the stairs.

'So as I was saying, I like...Bharaynatyama!' I said, realising that it was not the perfect time to tell her that!

Bharatnatyama? Like seriously? You like something you can't even spell right?

'Oh...That's great' she said with her perfect lips. I had half a temptation to kiss her. Maybe it was not the perfect time to show my manliness!

'I heard you dance well! Classical dance. You are performing at your annual day!' I said. Akshit's sister was in Mahira's class. Akshit was 'Behenpecked'. Like a husband who dances to his wife is called 'Henpecked', he danced to his sister's tune. I came to know these things from him earlier this day.

'Yes. It is tomorrow. I am excited! So much excited!' She said rubbing her hands together, as we reached the ground floor.

'That's all you wanted to say' she said, suspiciously.

'Yes. Bye' I said.

'Bye' she said and started to walk away.

'Mahira!' I shouted from behind. She stopped and turned towards me, 'Best of luck for tomorrow!'

She smiled. A smile that just made me lose my balance. A smile that I always needed. A smile that made me forget whatever happened yesterday or maybe the past five years!

I kept smiling that night. I didn't sleep, this time checking her Instagram profile. I hugged my phone and smiled. A smile I needed...and the one I deserved too!

VII

As expected she rocked the annual day with her Bharatnatyama performance. She uploaded some pics and believe me, she looked far above from beautiful.

I decided to text her what I felt for her. It was three days after her annual day that I decided to do so.

I picked up my phone and firstly started my conversation as we always did.

Sharief_Malhotra: **Hi there!**

Mahi_bhatt_mb: **Hey**

I didn't wanted to text her straight away that I liked her. So I opted a smart way instead.

Sharief_Malhotra: You know what, Utsav thinks I like you! I mean like seriously?

I inserted some 'laughing' smiles so that I didn't appeared serious.

Mahi_bhatt_mb: Hahaha! Mohini, your forever crush hasn't died. Why will you like me?

Her text hurt me a little. Yes, everybody in the tuition knew my madness for Mohini. But I never told them that my feelings for them have ended a long ago.

Sharief_Malhotra: **Mohini is shit! The way she behaves, like she is the only girl in the world. I don't like her anymore, she screwed me!**

I pressed the send button and waited. I imagined my text must be a little awkward to see for her to see. Mohini was really shit! She screwed me for so much time. I smiled as I felt I took some revenge.

Mahi_bhatt_mb: **Uhh Oh. Don't worry. Every boy has to face one such girl in his life! You know...It happens**

And there it was again. Her favourite line, 'It Happens'. Sometimes she used this so very much, I thought she was the brand ambassador of 'Wild Stone'.

I had hit the bulls eye. I got her sympathy; though I wanted her love instead. I thought of my next step; when her text appeared.

Mahi_bhatt_mb: **GTG. Bye**

Sharief_Malhotra: **Bye**

I kept my phone aside and thought about how to tell her that I liked her. After 20 minutes of thinking, I picked up my phone and started texting her.

Sharief_Malhotra: **You know what, you are the first girl that I have started to like so much after Mohini!**

I pressed the send button but immediately regretted it. Why did I mention Mohini? Why did I compared her with Mohini?

I unsent the message. Thanks to Instagram, you can unsend messages provided before the person you sent it has opened it. Thank god she didn't see that.

I started to type another text, this time a little sensible.

Sharief_Malhotra: **You know what I have started to like you...**

I pressed the send button and put my phone aside. I got up from my bed and went out of my room. I saw the clock, it was three of the evening.

'Will you have lunch?' My mom said coming out of the kitchen as I sat on the sofa.

'Yes' I said as she went back into kitchen and brought the usual middle class lunch. Rajma rice!

I started to eat it. My mom sat on the sofa next to me.

'May I ask you one thing?' She said looking at me. *What does she wants to ask?*

'Yes' I said putting the spoon down for a moment.

'Is there a girl in your life?' She said as chills ran down my spine. *Did someone told her that? How does she know? Maybe she is confirming!*

'Maa you know I am not like that. I don't have anyone!' I said with a *main-duniya-ka-sabse-shareef-launda* expression

'Good. You need to keep studies as your priority. Just asked after seeing your changed habits' she said picking up the glass on the table and sipping water from it.

'Changed habits? As in what?' I enquired.

'You have become a little more...what do we call that... sophisticated maybe. You nowadays keep staring in the mirror, spray perfume like mad and keep a good fashion sense. Last year you wasn't like this' she said.

Yes, she was right. I never cared for my fashion statement ever in my life. Whatever that was available, I wore that. But nowadays, I wore only what I liked. I kept a Mohawk hairstyle too, which was a little unusual of me.

I shook my head and picked up the spoon to eat again.

I went back into my room. An unknown feeling ran through my body. I was excited but feared too, at the same time. I was an atheist; but this time I wished Mahira from god. The funniest thing about humans is that we modify our habits and beliefs according to our needs!

I opened my Instagram. There was a message. I crossed my fingers and opened it.

Mahi_bhatt_mb: **So this means Utsav was right!**

I needed a 'How to understand a girl's text' guide right now. What does this mean? A yes? A no? Friend zoned? Of course, the most confusing thing on earth is a 'girl's text'. Nobody can understand them. Just like my handwriting!

Sharief_Malhotra: **I guess...**

Mahi_bhatt_mb: **Ahem ahem...**

What should I text now? 'Do you have cold?', 'will you have some water?' Or 'please tell me straight away what you want girl!'.

I decided to play it cool.

Sharief_Malhotra: **I guess this is absolutely normal**

I inserted some smiles. This is the usual strategy girl's have. Use smilies so that they neither appear too much interested nor they look as if they give a fuck about you!

Mahi_bhatt_mb: **Yes it is!**

Now my main question!

Sharief_Malhotra: **Do you like me as a person?**

She saw it. And exactly after fifteen point three four seconds her reply came.

Mahi_bhatt_mb: **Yes. I like you as a person; I just love your nature!**

Believe me, I danced like a madman at that time. I sang random romantic songs and held a pillow in my arms, making it dance with me too.

I picked my phone and kissed it.

Sharief_Malhotra: **Thank you so very much! I also love your nature! Bye**

Mahi_bhatt_mb: **Bye**

Well; frankly speaking I didn't understood what she meant by saying 'I like you as a person'. Maybe I was friend zoned. I compared myself to my friends. Of course; I was smarter than them and looked better too. So there was no chance of me getting 'Friend zoned'.

I wanted to know what she meant. All my female friends were busy. All my male friends; as expected were not able to get her too. So I decided to do what stupid people do. Google it.

I opened Google and typed 'What does she means when she says "she likes you as a person" ' and clicked the first result. It was a thread. The first answer was from a female and believe me; it crushed my happiness.

The girl wrote: "Maybe it is her polite way of telling you that she likes you only as a person. Not more than that. She isn't interested in a relation. She likes you as a friend!"

At that moment, I wanted to buy an assault rifle and shoot the hell out of that girl. I made a face and closed my laptop.

We had discussed relationships earlier too. She was of the view that couples do nothing but first fall in love, than fight all day and break up in the end. I never kept the same views for a relationship. I wasn't like the other boys, who bang a new chick every day. I believed in love.

I discussed this with my female friends in school. Their view was the one totally opposite to Google. They told me that she just meant what she texted. She meant that she likes me as a person; and nothing else.

I told my school friends about Mahira too. They were happy. Happier than me; for I forgot that Mohini. I kept talking about her to them. Sometimes I would discuss our texts with them. Sometimes one of my friend would say; 'bro, frankly speaking I heard the same thing about fifteen times for you only!'.

I was madly in love with her! Madly. I downloaded romantic songs. Shah Rukh Khan became my idol. I copied his way of talking, walking and whatever I could copy.

Though I appeared too much shy in front of her, I would prefer to text her over talking to her because: firstly I didn't had the courage to look straight at the most beautiful girl and second, whenever I looked at her; an urge to kiss her immediately dominated my mind. She got the perfect face, lips, eyes! How could one not think about kissing her?

In the next three months, I started texting her more than anyone else. One night, we chatted till three of the morning. I never texted anyone so much late. I started writing shayaries and posted them on my Instagram. I didn't care who liked it. The only like I waited for was hers.

The inspiration behind all my shayari's was her. She was the only thing I kept thinking of every second of my life. Even Mohini never had such an effect on me. Our texts started from 'Good morning' to 'How was your day?', 'had lunch/dinner', 'Aur batao' and end on 'Good night'.

I had decided to propose her. I kept the date of 31st December as final. Meanwhile, Utsav fell in love with my friend since sixth grade, Ayesha. Both of them loved each other. They came in a relation. That bastard surely changed a little. For now, he only came to school when she came. My other friends made me swear on my mother that if I make a girlfriend, I will never forget them.

I sat in the class, one normal day discussing my plan propose. It was 21st December. Only my squad was present in the class provided the rest of the class bunked.

You know this is the worst thing about high school! Singles and committed, bearded and shaved, fat and slim, tall and short, failures and toppers needed to survive it...that too together!

'So I am proposing her on 31st December' I addressed four people: Akshit, Utsav, Aryaman and Priyanshu.

'You know what...I think Mahira is also interested in you' Akshit said producing a comb out of his coat and combing his hair. Another involuntary action!

'How can you say that?' I said, puzzled. Priyanshu was busy eating my lunch from my lunchbox. He frankly gave a fuck about anything else other than Radhika; her crush and maybe food!

'I told you my sister is in her class. My sister asked her if she knows you. She told her that she is a very good friend of yours and said endless praises about you. Some were like "he takes poor kids to NesCafe" and all. You are a very good person and I think you deserve her. I saw her pic on facebook, should admit that she is beautiful!' He said gleaming at me. A wide smiled appeared at my face. I dreamed of floating into skies with her.

'Sharief' Aryaman shook me, 'bro you are seriously in love!' Laughing endlessly.

'Bro this is nothing. You need to look at him in the tuition! His one eye is on Mahira and the other on the black board! He has turned a laughing stock for others in the class!' Utsav said to Aryaman.

'Priyanshu what do you think? Should I propose her on 31st?' I said looking at him.

'I want to only say that…tell your mom add some sauce packet too in the box. Sandwiches taste good with sauce' he said. I gave him the finger and everyone started to laugh.

'31st is good. But there is a little risk in it' Priyanshu said.

'What risk?'

'If she says 'No'; your year will start with a 'no'. Things will become bad for you' he said as everyone agreed with him. I shook my head. He was surely right. Things were fifty.

'31st is final' I said more to myself and made a plan in my head, for the coming weeks. The first thing was to collect some money…To buy a gift for her!

Mahira Bhatt

Things between me and Sharief are going good.

Okay, so let me get this straight. Yes, I like him, but it's only as a friend. I know you people have been reading memes and jokes all over the internet where the girls troll the boys saying that they only like them as a friend but trust me, things are really different for girls.

Being in a relation means completely surrendering yourself to it. They say 'souls' come in relations not 'bodies'. It means that you'll devote all your time and soul to that particular person and unfortunately, I am not ready for all this.

Its not that I don't want relation with Sharief only. I don't really need a relation right now. I see that I am doing great in my life, my grades are high, my father and brother has high aspirations from me and I am happy. I don't really feel the need for a relation right now. You must be wondering I missed my mother, you are right, I miss her every day.

On the other hand, I know he's mad for me. All the shayaries and short stories he's been writing, contains some or the other hidden message for me. It's really cute sometimes.

I don't really want to hurt him by rejecting him. He had told me his whole story, how much he loved Mohini, how she threw him out of her life and how much fucked up he felt after she left him. I didn't wanted to see him in pain anymore. Though the naked sword with 'PROPOSE' written on it in bold and capital is just hanging above my head attached to a lose string and may fall of any time.

The truth is that I don't want our unnamed yet cute relation to end due to some complications. That's it.

My chains of thoughts were broken as my cousin just opened the door. She was in a red tee and shorts. She looked extremely pretty.

'Long time!' I said.

'Yes. Long time Miss Bhatt' she said and hugged me tight. I entered her home and sat on the sofa. She switched of the TV that played one of those useless teenage love triangle plot show.

'Like seriously?' I said, rolling my eyes. She laid back on the sofa. Her eyes were swollen and she looked extremely tired. Though she was of my age, she looked a little mature.

'How's uncle and bhaiya?' she said with her eyes open just a little.

'They are great. Keep asking "when will Smriti come to our home" This has become a routine' I said and passed a disappointing look. She had just visited her house five times in the past seven years.

'Studies and all. I am really sorry. Things with Rahul were also not going good' she said as I raised an eyebrow.

'What happened? You two still together naa?' I asked. She and Rahul were in a relation since the past two years. Both of them complimented each other and looked perfect.

'Yes we are good now but I don't think we could have if...' she paused and giggled.

'What?' I said as it felt like she had injected me with 'curiosity' that was in my blood and flowing to every part of my body now.

'Long story' she said. I let out a breath.

'Don't act like you are from one of the Chetan Bhagat books. Tell me else I leave' I said standing up.

'Sit. I'll tell you' she said. I sat back. She stood up and disappeared into the kitchen.

Five minutes later, she came back with a tray having two glasses of Pineapple juice and a bowl full of nachos.

'Looks like a really long story' I said as she got my sarcasm.

In the next fifteen minutes she narrated me how she went on a random date with a guy, weeks ago, just to make Rahul jealous and how the guy helped her being okay with Rahul again when she was thinking that he was cheating her and they were on the verge of 'Breaking Up'. The boy told her that she should talk and sort things out with Rahul and not suppose things herself. Things became real sweet when Rahul wasn't cheating on her and was instead planning a surprise birthday party for her!

'That's really cute and nice!' I said. She blushed.

'What's the name of that guy?' I asked.

'Nah! I won't tell!' she said.

'Okay. So don't tell me' I said.

'How's your life? Found a date? Oh...wait. Whom am I kidding. Mahira Bhatt found a date is impossible' she said as we laughed out loud.

'There's no date. But there's a boy' I said as all those tiring expressions disappeared from her face the moment she heard it. It literally looked like she had just been supplied with some glucose!

'BOY?' she shouted. Her voice echoed in the empty room.

'Yes. Boy' I said.

'He told me he likes me and I think he might be proposing me any moment. It feels really cute when I am with him. He writes Shayaries for me! Imagine' I said, blushing.

'That's damn cute! So? What's the problem?' she said.

'I don't really know if I want a relation or not. Like seriously, I am confused as hell' I said.

'Since how much time do you know him?' she said.

'Um...Past seven months' I said recalling dates.

'Give it some time. Know him properly first, only then you should think of getting into a relation' she said.

She was right! I should really give it some time!

'You know, he's really cute and he does these good work of helping poor people. I literally have never met such a guy before' I said.

'Yes. From your words, finding a boy like him in today's world is impossible. What if he's faking it?' she said.

'Faking it?'

'Like just doing this to get into your good books. What if he's not at all like that. Just a fake personality. Nobody is that good nowadays, Miss Bhatt' she said.

What does she mean?

'What should I do now?' I said. She had worsened my confusion.

'Give it some time. That's all' she said.

'Wait here. I'll order a pizza' she said and stood up. She left for her room leaving a totally confused soul behind.

My phone bleeped. It was a message from Ayesha.

"Sharief's going to propose you soon!!!! So happy for you both!!" the text read.

The sword unfortunately had fallen off.

VIII

I collected money for almost a week. The main sources of funds were: my pocket money, some borrowed from friends and some taken from mom (the reason being buying a new novel).

I sat on the sofa and saw the calendar. It was 28th December.

Three more days

I opened the box in which I kept the money and started to count.

'One thousand five hundred and thirty bucks' I said after four minutes of counting. Suddenly my phone rang.

It was from Mahira.

Why is she calling me?

I picked it up.

'Hello' her energetic voice greeted from the other side. A smile appeared on my face the instant I heard her voice.

'Hello Mahira. How are you?' I said, laying back in the sofa relaxing a little.

'I am fine. Hey, I want to ask you one thing' she said. Her voice sounded a little stressed.

'Yes' I spoke, my heart beating a little faster.

'Are you going to propose me?' She said as all the catabolic as well as anabolic reactions inside my body stopped. I froze.

How does she knows that?

Who told her this?

'Who told you this?' I said, letting out a breath.

'Its not about who told me this. Are you going to propose me?'

'Ahh. Yes' I said in reflex.

Damn! I should have thought some diplomatic answer for it Diplomacy works only in politics Mr Malhotra, not in Love.

'Look Sharief; I see you as a friend' she paused 'a good friend.'

A girl telling you she sees you as a 'friend' is like a large game over sign flashing in a video game

'You see; hearing this from a third person did hurt me a little. But please don't propose me. You are my good friend. I don't want to see you hurt…You listening?' She said in a calmer tone.

'Y…Yes I am hearing' I said; 'Okay so I won't propose you.'

'Good. And that person also mentioned Mohini to me. Said that 'I care for Sharief' and 'I don't want him hurt again' This is our matter. We can solve it ourselves. No need to bring a third person between' she said, 'bye.'

'Bye' I said as she hung up.

Who the hell told her this? Who can be that person?

One by one I started to recall my past days. Days when I discussed Mahira with my friends. None of my squad member was directly in contact with Mahira. Only Akshit's sister was in the same school as hers. But he could never do this…Then who?

The two idiots inside me appeared again.

'So how does it feels to be friend zoned Mr Malhotra? I told you…' *My idiot side said sharply and rudely.*

'She didn't friend zone you. She cares for you. That's why she told you not to propose her' the intelligent side, cutting the other in mid sentence.

'Oh yes. "You would be hurt" What does she means when she says you would be hurt? It is a straight NO. NO flashing in red and capital letters' the idiot said slapping the intelligent one on face.

'He will keep demotivating you' the intelligent side said.

'Please. I have had enough of this!' I said in air as both of them disappeared.

Not being able to propose a girl after so much wait and excitement hurts as much as when the sand castle you were making from the past few hours gets struck by a large tide!

'Mom, I need to go' I said, standing outside her room.

'Where?' She said, opening the door.

'I have some work to do. Will come home late' I said as she nodded.

I tucked the money in my pocket and sat in my car. The driver looked at me unexpectedly.

'Where to?' He said.

Just keep driving...

I was broken from inside. I was jealous of Utsav, because he had a better love life than me. Hey wait a second.... Utsav's girlfriend Ayesha is friend with Mahira (as we are in the same tuition). Can it be her? She already cares for me so much. I was lost in my own world when the driver again asked.

'Where to sir?'

'Rahul bhaiya. Is there an orphanage nearby?' I asked him as he smiled.

'Yes' he said

'Take me there. I have something to donate' I said as I heard the ignition of engine.

It took us twenty five minutes to reach there.

'Aasra: The shelter' read the board outside. I signalled my driver to sit in the car. I entered the building, still thinking who told Mahira that I was going to propose her.

The building was small. Walls needed white wash. Noise pollution was on its peak as kids were running around and making noises. An old man sat on a chair next to a table in a corner holding a pen in his hand.

'Namaste' I said as I sat next to him.

'Namaste ji. Tell me how may I help you?' He said in English. It was a little awkward for me to see an old man speaking English.

'Actually I am here to give some money' I said, taking out the crumbled notes out of my pocket. He raised an eyebrow.

'Alone?' He said as I straightened the notes with my palm. My mind was multi tasking at once. It was busy in finding the culprit, getting over the pain of being 'friend zoned' and feeling a little proud over my charitable act.

'Yes. Is that a problem?' I said.

'No. No problem. In my thirty five years, I have never seen a little kid like you alone coming here and donating money for a good cause. God bless you my son' he rose from his chair and patted my back. I felt a little happy.

I handed him the notes. Without counting them, he put them inside a drawer and stood up.

'Let's introduce you to the kids' he said exiting the room. I followed him.

He spoke how his father opened this orphanage to help kids live a better life. How he now has taken over the responsibility to fulfil his father's dream and various good deeds they do to serve the orphans.

'Kids! Kids' he spoke heavily, clapping in air. In a few seconds there was complete silence.

'This is our new friend. What's your name beta?' He looked at me

'Sharief'

'Oh. So you got a new brother, Sharief' he said as everyone clapped. I smiled after looking at those kids. Their clothes though a little torn were pressed and clean. Of course, the old man was doing his job.

'I have a little work to do. You can talk to them' he said patting my shoulder and leaving.

For the next forty five minutes I played with them.

'Bhaiya do you have a girlfriend?' A little girl maybe eight years old said.

'No' I shook my head and laughed 'someone told her that I was going to propose her before I did'.

'Haw. Who told her that?'

'Don't know'.

'It must be a girl. You know girls; we have a natural issue with hiding secrets' she said and I laughed. Her age was not matching the level of maturity she had attained.

Maybe she was right. It was Ayesha, who told Mahira about my plan.

You see that's why they don't have any women in RAW. Because they can't hide secrets!

My driver came inside. He looked a little worried.

'What happened' I asked him.

'Sir you said five minutes. It has been an hour since then' he said as I apologised to him. No one can keep record of time with kids!

I waved a good bye to everyone. All the kids waved their hands in air and smiled.

'Thank you beta' the old man said.

'Welcome uncle' I said sitting in my car.

I took out my phone and called Ayesha. To my horror, I was right. She told Mahira.

'You know Sharief, I have seen you broken when Mohini screwed you. I didn't wanted you to be screwed again' she said.

She was right. I was *screwed* by Mohini. I was left broken. I couldn't blame her; after all she cared for me.

'That's okay' I said; 'just control yourself a little next time please.'

'I will…I will' she said as I could sense her smiling on the other side.

'Bye!' I said and hung up.

And my fate to say; the new year's eve passed just like a normal day. The only difference being that I had a comment on my post 'The year has ended. So I would like to ask you one thing, what am I to you?' That read 'Cutest guy with awesome nature' from the girl I loved.

* * *

I loved January. Not because it was the start of the year. Not because it was the start of winters. But because I had my birthday!

I discussed being friend zoned with my friends. They assured me that it was absolutely normal which I didn't believe.

The situation in the class resembled like a war zone meeting room. Everyone was thinking their fucking brains out. The atmosphere was really damn cold. One could easily hear the joker saying, 'Why so serious?'

'You know when you are friend zoned, there is still a five per cent chance. I have been 'bro-zoned' twice. Bro-zone is like the worse. It leaves less chances than the bacteria that remain on a surface after being washed with Dettol' Priyanshu said breaking the long silence. His example of 0.01 per cent bacteria didn't go well with me.

'You see; this is the ultimate world. Girls use boys and when boys want commitment 'I like you as a friend' appears out of nowhere' Aryaman said, more worried than me.

'Our bro will get another good girl!' Akshit said, to cheer me up.

I ignored them. I had something else cooking in my mind.

Being a fan of the 'Fifty Shades of grey' series, I had an idea in mind. I would propose her on my birthday. Just like Christian Grey did. Maybe she will agree to it! I had my birthday on 25th January.

I know you people are wondering 'See how much desperate this guy is. Even after being friend zoned, he still wants to give it a try again'. You see being an Indian is the main reason behind this thinking. We keep visiting government offices for pensions, and one fine day we might get that. We keep Googling the latest I Phone's price even though we know its Aukaat ke bahaar. And what more, being a Punjabi makes it even more worse!

I didn't tell anyone about my birthday propose other than Pranav, my friend. I had told him to arrange a rose for that day.

I was chatting with her like we always did. It was 11:50 PM of the 24th January.

Mahi_bhatt_mb: **Good night :D**

What? Good night? Had she forgot about my birthday? This cannot happen!

I was shaken and a little more broken (more than being friend zoned). I made a face and typed a reply.

Sharief_Malhotra: **Good night**

I kept my phone aside as my family looked at the cake just like the terrorists from ISIS see the refugees captured, who are just about to be beheaded!

It was exactly 11:57 when I received a text

Mahi_bhatt_mb: ***Okay...so its tym to wish you "Happy Birthday" May god bless you. Happy year ahead!***

A lot of smilies were attached with it. She also made a collage of my posts from Instagram that had a Batman logo too in it.

I was just flattened. I never thought that someone would care so much for me. She was the first one to wish me. Even though she wished me four minutes earlier, I felt happy. I wide, wide big wide smile appeared on my face as I again saw the collage she sent.

Sharief_Malhotra: **Aww...Thank you so so so very much. Why did you texted me 'Good night' earlier?**

Mahi_bhatt_mb: **Because I had to make that collage. Your welcome :) Good night**

I texted her good night and cut the cake. I received calls and messages from Akshit, Utsav, Divi, Aryaman and many more. Ayesha uploaded a pic with me on her Instagram wishing me birthday. Utsav made a collage and posted it. It was seriously the best birthday start ever!

My birthday comes at such a time; when you can't party! Due to security reasons for the Republic Day; all the malls, restaurants were on high alert. I didn't felt a need to celebrate it that day with my friends. I picked up the date of 27th January. The date when I will propose her too.

What if she says no to me?

What if she rejects me?

What if she starts ignoring me and throws me out of her life just like Mohini did?

I stood in front of the mirror and practised random proposal steps. I bent on my knees, well it didn't work quite well. I tried uttering 'I Love You' in maybe thousand ways but every time I said it, it lacked self-confidence.

Freshly shaved, I dressed into the new grey coloured jacket I had purchased just last week. I applied some gel on my hair and some perfume too.

It was my day!

I called my friend Pranav.

'Hello' he picked up the call at the third ring.

'Sharief' I said.

'Oh yes. I am coming. Bahu Plaza, right?' he said.

'Yes. Right. Can you do me a favour?' I said.

'Yes. Why not' he said.

'Can you please bring a rose...' I said as he let out a laugh.

'Like seriously?'

'Yes. Please. Some important work' I said.

'Okay' he said, 'I surely will'.

He disconnected the call. I called Mahira.

'Sharief' she said with the most wonderful voice in the world!

'Yes. Mahira can you please come to Dominos today? I mean in the evening?' I asked, my heart on a treadmill.

'Um...We have our class right?' she said after a few seconds.

'I have told my friends I am going to introduce you to them. Please don't turn this down...Please' I said.

'Okay! I will come. But just in the recess time. I hope its okay with you?'

Okay with me? I was dancing in the heavens right now!

'Y…Yes. Absolutely okay with me' I said in the most fakest tone possible.

'Catch you later!' she said.

'Bye' I said and hung up.

The stage was set now. It was me who now had to perform. Alone.

I sat in the car gazing at my phone and thinking about the consequences. I wish I had a time machine that could tell me my future. I didn't want to be the richest person on earth. Nor I wanted to be called as a 'Legend'. I just wanted to hear those three alphabets. 'Y.E.S', that's all.

How we put our whole life on stake just for the sake of those three alphabets itself deserves a bravery award.

The driver smiled at me.

'Dominos' I said.

I had vowed that if she will say a 'No', I'll never order a Dominos Pizza ever. Like fucking ever!

There was a huge traffic jam. I checked my watch, it was two fifty five. The weather was cool, my brain wasn't. Right now it was more over heated than those cheap laptops which you need to place at a cool pad every time.

Maybe I was just over reacting. So what if she rejects me, I am still a good person. Well, I am not a good person but still… Rejection is never the end of the world.

The continuous honking of cars made me even worse. I opened the door and waved my middle finger at all the drivers who were pressing those god damn horns. They stopped at that very instant.

It took me half an hour to reach there. I waved a goodbye at my driver and he sped off. I stood outside Dominos. It was the place where I usually ate junk with my family, shared adult jokes with friends and flirted with random girls. It was a different place this time though.

I ordered a small coke for myself and sat on a table, staring at my phone. There was still much time to go. My friends would be arriving in another half hour. I started playing Candy Crush on my phone as the people on the neighbouring table passed disappointed looks to me.

'*Baccha hi rehna saaley*' I heard a male voice and a felt a smack right on my back. It stung like a bee. I knew who it was, from the intensity of slap.

'Guntas!' I said as I turned to him and hugged him tight. He was wearing a black sweater with the 'Batman' logo printed on it.

'You look sexy' he said and smiled.

'I hate that word' I said and frowned. Sexy was something that only cheap, mean and tards used. Just like Diveesh.

'Fuck. I know why that is so! Leave the past now. You told that Bhaabi is going to come today' he said and sat next to me.

'Please don't call her Bhaabi. She'll not be comfortable with it' I said as Divyam and Pranav just entered. Divyam held a cake in his hand.

'Happy birthday lala!' He said and made mad faces.

'Thank you'

'Bhaabi?' Pranav said.

This was why I wasn't inviting Mahira to the party because I knew that even if she had nothing to do with me; she would have been tortured till death by the infinite use of the word 'Bhaabi'.

'She'll come' I said and raised an eyebrow. 'I hope you got what I wanted.'

'Yes sir' he said and produced a red rose from the pocket of his jacket. The rose was absolutely amazing and it smelt way damn nice!

'Told that guy to spray some love' he said and chuckled.

One by one, everyone was there. We ordered many pizza's and ate them like mad men. I waited for the time that would decide my happiness. Well, that for now was Six o'clock.

It was five fifty five. All the money I had brought was over by now, thanks to the insatiable stomach my friends have got.

'Where's she man?'Akshit said, his mouth stuffed.

I took out my phone and called her. She didn't respond.

'She must be coming. Wait' I said and relaxed on the chair.

'Lets have some kind of entertainment before she comes' Guntas said and walked slowly towards me.

I knew what he was up to.

Before I could have even thought of some exit plan, my specs were removed and my face was dabbed with chocolate cake. Not only my face, it was all over my jacket. They clicked random selfies with my cake laced appearance.

I went to the washroom accompanied by Karanveer and Aryaman. Both of them tried to clean the living shit out of my jackets and face. Though my face was normal again, my jacket still smelt of chocolate. I shook my head as I saw myself in the mirror.

I fished out my phone and again called her. She didn't respond again. It was six ten. Ten minutes above the deadline. I kept calling her again and again but still, there was no response.

Maybe she got a hint that I was going to propose her and that's why she preferred not to show up!

I mentally kicked myself. Everything around me turned black and white. It felt worse than watching a Sajid Khan movie. It felt like my head was going to burst now. I had happily screwed everything!

Heavens showered blessings and the god turned to favour, as I saw her emerging from the other block of the corridor. Dressed in a red T-shirt, that had flowers printed on it and a blue jeans, she looked amazingly, god damningly, awestruck beautiful!

I froze the moment I saw her. The reactions in my brain stopped mid way.

'She's here' I said more to myself. Words failed to reach their eyes.

'What?' all of them said.

'She's here' I repeated, a little louder this time.

In just two minutes, my hairs were set, my jacket was cleaned and I was forcefully sprayed with four sprays of a mouth freshener. I couldn't believe my friends cared so much for me.

She stood behind the door. She was with a friend of hers, Mansi.

Mansi was thrice the size of Mahira. She was heavy, tall, boyish and acted like she was a bouncer.

'Let's go outside' I said as all of them stood up and followed me outside.

'Hi!' she said and brought her hand closer to mine. We shook hands and it sent electric signals down my spine!

'H…I' I said, with my mouth open.

'Just wanted to introduce you with my friends' I said, 'Guys, this is Mahira. The girl I keep talking about' I said and she blushed. I wasn't lying. She was the only girl I kept talking about.

She waved at my friends. One by one, all of them said their names. It felt like a major throwback to the first day of sixth. She smiled.

I was pushed away to a dark corner by my Karanveer. Though he was a little sardar, rough work out had made him equally as powerful as me.

'The girl…' he said.

'Mahira' I said.

'Yes. Mahira. She's damn pretty' he said and blushed.

'As if I never knew this' I said and rolled my eyes, 'why did you brought me here?'

'Propose her' he said.

'Will she say 'Yes'' I said, my brain as dull as the lightning in the corner.

'Of course she will. And even if she doesn't, I am here. A substitute for her' he said and held my hand playfully. I slapped his back and went back to my friends who now were laughing with Mahira like they knew her from the beginning. I started to feel jealous.

'Wait. I'll bring the pizza's' I said as I disappeared inside the food joint and returned back with three pizzas, I had bought for my tuition mates.

'Here' I said as I gave them to Mansi. She stared at the carry bag like she had an X-Ray vision.

'Can we leave now?' Mahira said with her perfect lips.

'Y…Yes' I said, my heart beating fast and all the faces of my friends falling. I was surely letting the love of my life walk away.

She smiled and turned away and walked slowly. Or maybe it was my mind that was making it slow motion. I could literally feel my heart just jumping out of my chest and running behind her.

I was a loser. I admit.

Stop her, you idiot!

Stop her!

Stop her!

Stop your Love!

'Mahira!' I shouted from behind. She was just three steps away from me. She turned towards me.

I went a little close to her, our breaths meeting. I took out the rose from the front pocket of my jacket and handed her.

She stood still, blushing confused, random expressions passing by her face, looking at the rose.

'Please' I said as my friends hooted.

Please? Like what are you offering her, some policy? Some money? Some food? No you god dam nit! You are offering her your heart...and please?

She took the rose and smiled at me.

'I love you' I said as she blushed and started to move.

'I love you too' Mansi said and chuckled. Thank god Dominos got no knives in their kitchen. Else, I would have committed a murder today.

All my friends started to praise about Mahira. How she was beautiful and cute. Endless praises. I slapped all of them with only one sentence. "I know that, right?"

In another hour, all of them left. Only I, Akshit, Anirudh, Priyanshu and Aryaman remained. We went to a park nearby and sat there till my tuition got over.

I saw her coming through the stairs. All my friends congratulated me for my birthday. Some from the other batches complained that they didn't get to eat the pizza.

Our eyes met and she smiled at me. She didn't utter a single word, just kept walking with her friends.

What is this?

A Yes?

A No?

God!

I had to wait for her to reach her home and come online. And believe me, they were the longest seventeen minutes and twenty three seconds of my life!

IX

Mahira Bhatt

I held the rose in my hand and walked slowly back to my class. Mansi giggled and kept poking me again and again. Though I was annoyed at her, I was a little happy too. I had seen it coming. I knew why he had called me to the party, in front of his friends.

That propose was cute. Like seriously. Imagine a cake laced guy who smelt of chocolate standing just few inches away from you, giving you a rose and telling you that he loves you. I smiled as I replayed that moment in my head.

'What do you think?' I asked Mansi.

'What do I think? Does it matters? What you think matters! I think he really loves you' she said, her eyes still on the pizza carry bag.

'Should I say yes.'

'Only if you love him, say yes. Think about it. It's not a 'Who wants to be a millionaire' question that has a certain time limit. Follow your heart' she said.

Follow your heart, three words. Just three. What nobody can ever imagine is that sometimes these three words give you immense pain and a lot of tears. I wasn't ready for following my heart...again.

Two Years Ago

'Is he cute?' Ridhima said. She held that photo so tightly, folds started to appear on it.

'He is. Kind of' I said and opened my maths textbook.

'He asks me about you. Everyday' she whispered slowly as we had caught the attention of the maths teacher and he stared us like he had seen us on the front page of a newspaper just this morning.

'Shut up' I said.

'His name is so cute' she said and blushed.

From the past two weeks, she has eaten all of my brain telling me that a boy keeps asking her about me. The boy lives next to her house and had seen me when one day, I had gone to her home, I showed no interest in either hearing about the boy from her or in Mathematics. Right now, my mind was totally fucked up.

'I don't want to hear it' I said and slapped her arm.

'At least talk to him once. Please. He's dying to' she said.

'And what exactly do you want me to tell him' I snapped.

'Date Ridhima. That's all' she said and I rolled my eyes. She was insane.

Some girls in our school went gaga over each and every boy they ever met. I repeat, only some. Ours is a 'Girl's only' school. Most of us don't even have a boy friend. We are happy, in a world of our own, where there's no formality and gender equality bullshit. On the other hand, there are some girls of our school that have set an aim. The aim is to make 100 boyfriends. They literally crave for boys. I hate them.

I am not one of them. Things are happy for me. They call me the 'Smile' for I keep smiling each and every time. This is the secret mantra of my life. Smile when happy, smile when sad, everything will be all right, nothing remains forever bad!

I never felt the need of a boyfriend. Though I have boyfriends but boyfriend, that's a really different case. Its a pathetic thing to talk or even think about for me.

The maths class ended and the bell rang. It was the start of summer vacations!

No matter how many exclamatory marks you put after "summer vacations", they always disappoint you and leave you bored, alone and a little madder.

I picked up my bag. Isha, was absent today so I had to go alone. Ridhima stared at me and expected me to say something.

'What?' I said after looking at her expressions for a second.

She made a puppy face. The one that a puppy makes at a pet shop when you have to choose between two puppies. That face. The face of hope, light, love and utter bullshit.

'I'll think about it' I said.

'Why can't you come today?' she said.

'I said that I am going to think about it. By the way, from where did you got that photo of his?' I said.

'Sneaked in his home' she said and giggled. I rolled my eyes.

I started to walk to my home. Alone this time.

'How was the day!' My brother said the moment I entered the home.

'Boring' I said.

'What happened?' he said, his expressions serious. This is where Indian brothers lack sometimes. They become serious for every small thing that concerns their sister.

'Isha was absent' I said.

He let out a laugh.

'What?' I said in an annoyed tone.

'Nothing. Your friend called' he said.

'Which friend?'

'Ridhima' he said. I let out a breath.

'And what exactly did she say?' I said.

'Invited you to come to her home' he said and smiled, 'you can.'

'But I don't want to go' I said. His face fell.

I knew why his face fell. If I were not home, he could easily sneak outside and go to meet his girlfriend. Dad's busy with the office all the time. He'll hardly notice.

'Why?' he asked, a little hurt.

'She got no Wifi!' I said uttering the first thing that came in my mind.

He laughed again.

'Is that a problem? Problem solved' he said and produced an internet dongle from his jeans pocket.

I fake smiled. I had to go now and she'll make me meet that guy who is a bit cute.

'Go and change. We'll eat outside and I'll drop you at her home' he said. I nodded and went in my room for a quick shover and dressed in a black T-shirt and blue jeans. I looked in the mirror. I combed my hair and applied a little perfume.

I sat in the car and he started to drive. We stopped at Mc Donald's and had a burger and cold coffee there. In another fifteen minutes, we were there. He dropped me at the entrance of the lane. I waved at him. A bag full of night clothes hanged on my back. My plan was to stay for two days.

I walked slowly through the lane and felt a shadow behind me. I turned but there was no one. I shook my head and again started to walk. A shadow again crossed my path. I kept walking and didn't stopped. I turned my head in reflex and saw the same boy Ridhima was talking about standing there, in a green shirt and brown jeans.

'Hi!' he said and smiled wide.

'Before Hi and all, can I please ask you why are you stalking me?' I said in the most annoyed tone possible.

'I am really sorry. Well stalking is not my taste' he said in a perfect accent. There was something very Christian Grey about him. The way he talked, they way he looked, white, tall and freshly shaved.

'You better be' I said. His face fell.

'Mahira, can we be friends?' he said after a short pause.

'No! We can't! I don't even know your name!' I said and started walking.

'Only if the name is a problem, Raghav' he said from behind. He was surely an idiot. I didn't turned back and kept walking until I reached her home.

Once I was standing in front of the main gate of her house, I scanned the area again to look for that desperate yet cute creature. I unzipped my bag and took out Pepper spray in case of an emergency. After examining it a little, I kept it back inside and clicked the bell thrice.

'Here you are' she said the moment she saw me. I passed a disappointing look.

'What?'

'That desperate creature…Raghav…he followed me!' I gasped in horror.

'You must be lying!' she said, 'he's inside'

'Fuck! Then who was that guy?' I asked her, confused. He knew my name too.

'Don't know. Lets go inside' she said and offered to take my bag. I declined and stepped inside her home.

Her home reminded me of the homes in those old Sanskari movies. A tulsi plant right in the centre of the home and a large banyan tree in the corner. Birds cooed, wind blew touching my face gently and everything was so quite.

'Namaste aunty' I said the moment I saw her mother.

'Namaste beta. Ridhima had told me about you. You must be Muskaan, right?' she said.

'No…no aunty. I am Mahira' I said as she rolled her eyes at her mother.

'You disappoint me. Always!' she said, 'lets go to my room.'

'But beta…' her mother said as she cut her mid sentence.

'Please maa' she said and walked into her room and banged closed the door.

'I am sorry aunty' I said. Though she was my friend, she was wrong.

'Its okay beta…Kids nowadays only realise the value of something once its gone. Even a mother' she said and let out a breath.

I froze. I could feel her pain. She was hurt.

'MAHIRA!' She shouted from her room.

'Got to go, aunty' I said and folded hands. I opened the door and startled.

Raghav was sitting right next to her on the sofa. It was the same guy who was stalking me. The same idiot who I think looks like Christian Grey.

Both of them were laughing and stopped the moment they saw me.

'Is this how you behave with your mother?' I snapped at Ridhima. She became red.

'She deserves that' she said. Raghav looked at both of us, confused.

'Just have a look at her age. She does so many things for you, from day to night, keeps herself so busy and after so many things, you expect her to remember your friend's name? Unbelievable' I said in the most harsh tone possible.

Her face fell and she became more red.

'I…am…sorry' she hardly managed to speak with tears full in her eyes, ready to shoot.

I hugged her tightly. She was my best friend and I had to give her a second chance. She hugged me back even more tighter.

Raghav clapped.

'And the Oscar for the best actor female, goes to Mahira Bhat!' he said and whistled.

'You Mr. You were stalking me a few seconds earlier and now, here you are, sitting in my friend's home just the next moment. What are you? Monkey man?' I said and laughed at my own joke.

'That's rude' he said, 'I am fast'

'Please' I said and looked away.

'Guys don't fight. Mahira, this is Raghav. Raghav' she said.

'Looks like your friend likes to stalk random girls' I said.

'Correction. Beautiful girls' he said and I don't know why but I smiled. He surely was a great flirt.

'Shut up' I said. He started to laugh.

'Looks like someone's really angry' he said.

I didn't replied. Her mother knocked at the door. I opened the door and saw her standing with a tray with three glasses filled to the top with mixed fruit juice. *Mothers!*

'Thought you must be hungry' she said and entered the room. She placed the tray on the table and before she could leave, Ridhima hugged her tightly and kissed her on the cheek.

'I am sorry Maa…I love you' she said. Her mother smiled.

'*Mahira ke saath reh kar acchi baatien seekh rahi hai'* she said and kissed her forehead. It looked like a scene from a typical Karan Johar movie. I wanted to whistle.

Raghav looked at me, with gleaming eyes.

'You are a really nice girl' he said.

'I know that. Thanks anyway' I said.

We sat on the sofa and talked endless shit. I think that our talks could even put a drunk guy to shame. From aliens, god, ghost, money, ambition, love to the prime minister of India and Ranveer Singh's body, it was our topic of discussion for the day.

After two hours of constant babbling, we laid down in the sofa and rested. I saw Ridhima almost snoring and Raghav still looking at my face.

'Mahira' he said.

'Lemme sleep naa…' I said in an irritated tone.

'Mahira…' he again said, a little louder this time.

'Hmm…'

'I love you' he said.

My eyes that were just centimetres open till now popped. My head went dizzy and it looked that I just smoked a pot.

What the fuck! He loves me? Like seriously?

'You are lying right…' I said.

'Look into my eyes' he said. I stood up and looked at him.

'I fell in love with you the moment I saw you for the first time. It was two months ago, when I saw you bargaining with Auto driver. You remember it right?' he said and it hit me with full force.

'And the driver didn't took money from me…Was it because of you?' I said in reflex.

'Yes. I really love you Mahira. It took me two fucking months to see you again. I was dying inside. Part of me exploding day by day. I am sorry for appearing a stalker to you but trust me, I couldn't wait anymore when I heard that you were coming' he said.

Wow. There's someone who cares for me on this earth. Someone who waited for so much time to meet me again! Someone who loves me.

'Does he really love you?' a voice asked inside me, 'how much time do you know him from. Two hours?'

'He really loves you! Are you blind! Can't you see the love for you in his eyes?'

'Mahira…Do you love me?' he asked.

How was I going to answer him.

What should I say?

A yes?

A no?

Give it some time?

Maybe think about it?

'Are you ready with the answer Mahira' he said. His eyes were melting now and even in the air-conditioned room, sweat beads started to appear on his face.

'What?' I asked out of context.

'Do you love me?' he said.

Here it goes. Three. Two. One.

'Yes' I said and smiled. He shouted loudly.

'OH MY GOD! I CAN'T BELIEVE THIS!' he said loudly. So loud that Ridhima woke up.

'What the fuck is going on here?' she asked, half asleep.

'Finally Ridhima. We are together!' he said.

'What?' she said now coming back to her senses.

'Yes. We are together' I said and smiled.

He looked at the watch on the wall.

'Got to go. Bye love' he said to me.

'Bye' I said and blushed. He really looked like Christian Grey with no romantic skills.

'Bitch' Ridhima said the moment he exited the room, 'I don't think relations are made for me'

'Shut up' I said.

'I don't believe this' she said and slapped herself so hard that a red spot appeared on her face out of nowhere.

'You know…it happens' I said and blushed.

I don't really think that giving relation a shot is a bad thing. Nobody is going to cry and write novels after break up after all. It happens in the movies. Only in the movies. Most of my classmates were now committed. Some with more than one guy. So what if I get into a relation?

In the next two days, we enjoyed a lot. We went to the cinemas to watch a romantic movie, had lunch in a restaurant and laid ourselves in a park in the sun shine. He was rich. He got contacts all over. Had it not been his contacts, we still would have been in the home eating the same pizza thrice.

He even took me to his home. He showed me his room. His home was twice the size of Ridhima's but thrice as peaceful. The whole house was decorated in Red. The walls, the ceilings, the fans, everything I could see was red.

These happy days unfortunately, ended way too soon for us the moment my brother came back to take me home again. I cried. I didn't wanted to leave him. He started to become the world to me. Funny how attachment even for two days is considered 'Love' and is so strong that it could even make you cry.

'Here. Take this' he said as he handed me a small piece of paper.

'What's this?' I said.

'My phone number. We can chat to each other. Distances can never separate love!' he said as my brother pressed the horn even harder outside.

'Bye love' I said and waved at him. I saw my brother dressed in a red T-shirt and black jeans.

'What happened?' he said the moment I sat in the car.

'What?' I said.

'No more "Bhai!!! I missed you"? What's with that sad face? Someone said something to you?' he said, 'Oh wait wait wait... Who wants' to get their bones broken by picking up a fight with Mahira?'

I laughed hard. So hard that my face landed on the dashboard.

'Now that's like my little dumb sister' he said and stepped his feet on the accelerator.

We texted each other a lot. Either I was doing my home work or texting him. It really felt so much special when someone skipped school just to talk to you the whole day. We laughed, we cried, we smiled, we said 'I love you' but most importantly we missed each other.

'Mahira! Mahira' my brother called me from upstairs.

'Yes' I said. I was downstairs, sitting in the lobby doing my homework.

'Its your phone!' he said.

'Whose that?' I asked him. I had saved Raghav's number as "Ridhima 2".

'Ridhima 2 calling' he said as I threw my notebooks aside and climbed the stairs as fast as possible.

I picked up the call.

'Hello?' I said. There was no voice from the other side.

'Hello?' I repeated. Still, there was no one there. Just random sounds of breathing,

'I tell you…She's a time pass' I heard a male voice say. In a fraction of seconds, I recognised who he was. It was Raghav.

The sound was low and disturbed. One could literally hear nothing, thanks to my super abilities of eaves dropping.

His phone must be in his pocket, I guessed. The voice appeared to be far from the phone.

'No baby. I really love you. It was you whom I saw first, not Mahira' he said as my heart broke to pieces with every word he uttered.

'But how can I cheat on my best friend?' a familiar female voice said. No doubt, it was Ridhima.

'We are not cheating. We are just exploring each other. Just getting to know each other. Me and Mahira are a different case. We are just attracted to each other, that's all. No love bullshit. You are my real love' he said as I hung up the call. I didn't wanted my heart to be broken any further. It was already into a million pieces.

I locked myself in the room and cried. I cried a lot. I wasn't the 'Smile' they used to call me. I felt weak and cheated, something I had never felt before. This is why I hate love. Sometimes the person who makes you believe in love is the same person who makes you hate it later!

'Miss Mahira Bhatt' Piyush sir said breaking my heavy chains of thoughts, 'can you please explain whatever we read today?'

'S…Sir…I am sorry sir' I said almost choking.

'Sorry for what?' he said.

'I…am …sorry…sir' I said as thankfully the bell rang at that very instant.

'Revise whatever we learnt today' he said and exited the class.

Utsav came to my desk.

'Mahira, here' he said as he placed a small pack of chocolates on my table.

'What? I can't take this! I protested.

'Its not from me. Its from…um…Sharief' he said and winked. I picked it up and placed in inside my bag. I smiled at the attempts that idiot in love does to make me smile.

I called Smriti the moment I exited the main building.

'He proposed me' I said in an unusually excited tone.

'Who?' she said equally excited.

'Sharief' I said as softly as possible.

'Sharief Malhotra? That Mohini guy? You serious? Where did you met him?' she said in one breath.

What the! How does she knows about him?

'How do you know about him?' I asked.

'Long story. Thank him from my side again' she said.

'Thank him? Why?' I asked confused as fuck.

'Little busy right now. I said "Long story". Just thank him. 'Bye' she said and disconnected the call.

X

My heart beat faster. Faster than Eminem's rap! In my car, I again checked if she was online. She wasn't.

What if she is disgusted at my cheap attempts of having a relation with her again and again?

What if she doesn't wants to see my face again?

My mind roamed searching for the questions as the car stopped and I was back home.

At that very moment, my phone bleeped. I took it out. A message from Mahira. I stood at the gate and opened her text.

Mahira_bhatt_mb: **Thank you for the chocolates! And for the rose too**

Chocolates? Where did this come from?

Suddenly it hit me that I had given Utsav a pack of small Ferero Rochers to give to Mahira.

Sharief_Malhotra: **Ohh! The chocolates. I completely forgot about them. I am sorry for that propose. It was the shitiest propose in the world one could ever do! xD**

I pressed the send button and regretted what I had done earlier this day.

Who the hell says 'Please' while giving flower to a girl? Couldn't I do it better? Like bending on my knees and then proposing her?

I had googled 'How to propose a girl' (I see a wide smirk appearing on your face now. Sorry but I have no experience with girls so I had to Google it). The first result was a website that made three things clear at first.

1. Never include a third person in your propose. It would feel like you lack courage.

2. Never propose on a text. Face to face proposes are the best!

3. Make it the best day of her life. Propose is something that a girl never forgets even after breakup.

I made a mental note to myself. I had done the first two things but was doubting if I had done the third thing or not. Obviously; a person holding a rose wearing a cake-laced jacket stammering 'Please' is never going to be the *best day of her life!*

Mahira_bhatt_mb: **No no. That was something...cute!**

Cute? Bulls eye!

Mahira_bhatt_mb: **I was actually anticipating something like that!**

Justin Bieber's 'What do you mean' rang in my head.

Sharief_Malhotra: **So what's your answer?**

I pressed the send button as at that instant my father came from inside, looking a little puzzled.

'You have been standing here for quite some time. Don't want to come inside? Fought with your mom?' He asked, still in his '*I have a red light on my car and I rule everyone*' clothes as well as look. I shook my head and came inside as he bolted the door behind me.

'How was your party?' He asked as I sat on the sofa, removing my jacket which smelt of chocolate though my idiot friends had tried enough to wash the cake off it.

'Amazing! Thank you dad' I said and hugged him. My dad is my superhero. Neither he has abilities to climb walls nor he can fly in the sky shooting ultra laser rays from his eyes. Yet; he fulfils my each and every wish without asking twice and we shared a special bond.

'Look at yourself. Thanking your dad? God what the world is coming to!' He said as I laughed.

My mom emerged out of her room.

'I told you to come home earlier. It is nine now. What's wrong with you?' She said as I threw a *please-mind-your-own-work* look at her. She ignored me and disappeared in her room again.

Me and my mom shared a very different relation. A little screwed up one. On some days we would fight with each other and on some days we would behave like we couldn't live without each other. Well it was all my fault, after that incident we were not the same as before. I loved my mom but sometimes hormones raged and I found myself shouting at her. I wish I had a time machine to go back to that day when…ah! Leave that.

'You are not again talking to her? Why?' My dad said, his eyebrows up.

'I am not answerable to her sometimes' I said and took out my phone again.

'If you are not answerable to the person who gave you birth, than to whom are you answerable Mr Malhotra?' He said in an angry tone; 'Sleep now.'

I stood up and entered my room, locking it from inside and deliberately banging the door hard.

I opened my Instagram.

Mahira_bhatt_mb: **Are you serious?**

Am I serious? No baby I was just playing a prank!

Sharief_Malhotra: **Of course, I am.**

Mahira_bhatt_mb: **Sharief look. I know you won't ditch anyone and you have a good heart. But please understand….**

I don't want to be in a relationship with anyone. You yourself told me that "these relations are shit and fake". Now you yourself want a relation. Why is it so? Please...I don't think I will be comfortable with a relation :D

My heart swell up and the pieces that remained after she kind of 'friend zoned' me were burnt to ashes. I wanted to cry and shout at her. Why can't she just agree?

Yes, I lied to her. That these relations are shit. I loved relations though I never entered one because in my view; I am the most pervert person on earth.

Imagine a guy being turned on by the view of street dogs making out in rain! I was a cheap low minded idiot though I never spoke shit about females.

Sharief_Malhotra: **Okay. Its okay :D**

Mahira_bhatt_mb: **You okay with it naa?**

You okay with it? Like how can someone be okay when friend zoned?

Sharief_Malhotra: **Yes Yes...I am**

I pressed the send button. She then texted me a 'Good night' to which I didn't reply.

I become unusually angry; don't know why. Hormones rushed through and I could break the face of anyone at that time.

At that time, I heard a knock at the door.

I opened it and saw my mom standing there with a plate of fruits in her hand.

'Thought you must be hungry. Have this' she said and brought that plate towards me.

'I DON'T WANT THIS! WHY DON'T YOU DO YOUR OWN WORK?' I shouted, loud enough for my neighbours to call the police. Tears appeared in her eyes. I said it in reflex.

'This is what I deserve! Who told me to bring food for you huh? Look at your face you…' she said as I cut her.

'Leave…please' I said, folding my hands.

'I won't leave! What will you do? Other than hitting your mother again?' She said, tears rolling down her face. I was a complete asshole to make my mother cry.

I stood there, staring the floor shamelessly and it hurt me as if she had slapped me. She left for her room and I closed the door again, sitting on the bed wide awake.

'She is right. What can I do other than hitting her? Again' I said to myself.

Two Years Ago

I washed my hands and face. I wiped them with a handkerchief afterwards. I was standing in the school washroom.

Two boys one short and one long; came inside, laughing and giggling. I shifted my vision as the short one of them took out a crayon from his pocket and scribbled

"Mohini Sharma is a Slut" and "Want to have sex with me? Meet me outside IX D"

I stood there motionless. Yes, I was hearing the rumours about Mohini being a slut or having sex with a college boy. Yet, I still loved her as much as earlier.

'This girl makes my cock go all the way up bro' the tall one said to the other who was busy staring the wall as if it was 'The Monalisa's painting'.

I clenched my fist. The two boys were older, bulkier and muscular than me. They could knock me down in one attempt. I kept quiet.

'She is like the new slut in town. Heard she gave a blowjob to that guy what's his name…Fuck! I can't recall his name. He is all rich, muscular and guess what they did it in his new car!' The other one finally spoke.

'Maybe she will have sex with us too! Both of us. We'll pay her whatever she wants. She is into rich and big boys and we are what she needs!' The tall one said as both of them high fived and left the washroom without urinating.

How can Mohini do this?

She is not like this! She is not a slut! She is my Mohini! My little angel! She can't do this.

I kept telling myself this as I ran towards my class IX D. I needed to talk to her. I collided with endless people, there was crowd as it was recess time.

I entered my class and saw Mohini sitting with the three of her best friends.

'Is it true what everyone is saying?' I asked her. She didn't reply. She stared in my eyes.

'I am asking is it true what everyone is saying? Did you slept with a…' I said as at that time one of her best friend cut me.

'It is none of your business! Its her life. She can do whatever she wants to. Who the fuck are you to ask her?' She said as I looked down.

'There are guys outside who want to sleep with you. They say you take money for such things. I can't believe them' I said more of cried.

'Leave them Sharief' she said as I settled on my seat and kept reminding myself that this is all a lie for the rest of the day.

'Oh…My beta is here!' My mom said opening the door. I was angry. Angry as hell. My insides burnt from the cold response Mohini had given to me. Maybe everyone is right!

I ignored her and kept my bag on the sofa and sat next to it; something unusual of me.

"Maybe we can sleep with her too" the words of those boys rang in my head. I wanted to slap the fucking shit out of them. Their words kept digging holes inside my heart every time I thought of them.

'What happened Sharief?' My mom asked. I didn't reply.

She went to the kitchen and came back with a glass of water in her hand. She offered me that.

I don't know why I did it but I did. I took the glass from her and smashed it right on the wall. Then I pushed her back and she was lying on the floor, looking at me, staring in my eyes, searching for her son. Her son Sharief.

'She didn't do anything like that!' I shouted angrily and disappeared in my room, she still on the floor rubbing her eyes. After that day, she never saw her son again. Maybe not in the way she did earlier....

I cried as old memories hit my hard. I turned my laptop to power and queued songs, collapsing in the bed to sleep.

I woke up to Lucky Ali's 'Tere mere saath' at two of the morning. I had heavy headache and my body burnt! I had high fever.

I removed my T-shirt and got out of my room. I saw my mother, reading 'Twilight' with that plate of fruits next to her on the sofa.

'Maa...Maa' I said, feeling a little nauseous.

'What happened?' She stood up immediately and rushed towards me. I vomited on the floor and collapsed on the ground...

* * * *

I woke up on my parents bed. My mom sitting right next to me with little dark circles under her eyes. She didn't slept and was sitting next to me for the whole night!

My eyes searched for dad. I looked at the clock, it was 11:00 AM.

'How are you now?' She finally said.

'My head hurts' I said as I placed my hand on my forehead. I felt a little privacy invaded as I wasn't wearing my T-shirt and was half naked.

'We need to go the doctor. Lets go' she said as I stood up, hardly able to balance myself and went in to the washroom for a shower.

We went to the doctor afterwards. He said that I just have caught cold and I need to wear warm clothes. My mom complained that I didn't heard her every time she told me to put warm clothes on and my my habit of eating ice cream at midnight without telling my parents.

The doctor prescribed me medicines and warned me. We left the clinic and drove home afterwards.

'Where are you going?' My mom said looking at me dressed in Blue Jacket and jeans.

'Tuition' I said.

'Tuition in such condition? No chance' She said.

'Sir is going to start a new chapter. Its important, I don't want to miss it' I lied and touched her feet to leave for my tuition.

Mahira saw me and smiled. I didn't. I myself regret the way I behaved that day. I had no expression on face, rushed out of the class as the bell rang for recess and didn't utter a single word for the whole time, holding my forehead as it hurt me bad.

After sometime, the tuition got over. The moment the bell rang, I picked up my bag and rushed out, ignoring any sort of eye contact with her.

'Sharief' her friend Shefali came to me; 'Mahira told me to tell you to come online.'

I nodded and sat in my car.

Mahi_bhatt_mb: **Are you okay?**

I frowned and typed a text.

Sharief_Malhotra: **Yes. Shefali told me that you wanted to talk. I am all here.**

Mahi_bhatt_mb: **You are not well?**

Is this what she wants to talk about?

Sharief_Malhotra: **Yes I am not well. My head rings. Is this what you wanted to talk about?**

Mahi_bhatt_mb: **No. Actually I wanted to talk about yesterday...Are you okay with it?**

The car stopped as I reached home. I entered the house, still typing.

Sharief_Malhotra: **Yes. Absolutely okay!**

Mahi_bhatt_mb: **I thought that we could come in a relation...But I don't have trust on myself...**

A wide smile, more wider than the LED in Ambani's house appeared on my face. Finally she is thinking not about 'her' but of 'we'.

It took me exactly five minutes to type a reply. It was large, large enough for Instagram to declare itself as a blogging website. It went like this.

Sharief_Malhotra: **Look, let me get things straight. I am not a person who craves for a relationship. If I wanted only a relation, I would have had it long ago but no. I believe in love. Its all up to you. If you don't want a relation, its okay. If you want a relation then also its okay. The only difference is that being in a relation will make me a little more happy (as little as the universe). You decide. No pressure, all up to you!**

I breathed heavily as her text appeared.

Mahi_bhatt_mb: **Okay! *As little as universe* xD**

Justin Bieber's 'what do you mean' rang in my head again.

Sharief_Malhotra: **I await your reply...**

Then a reply came that felt like a bomb named 'happiness' dropped on my head.

Mahi_bhatt_mb: **Yes**

It was an amazing feeling! Finally she agreed! The world felt different. The air smelt different. There was more sweetness in the air now. I felt as if I lost my virginity. I smiled and smiled again.

Sharief_Malhotra: **I still didn't get it. Is it a yes?**

I sent just to be double sure.

Mahi_bhatt_mb: **Yes. Good night <3**

I replied her a good night and kissed my phone. Yes, kissed my phone though it tasted more of 'surface cleaning liquid'.

I knocked at my parents room. They were unaware that half hour has already passed and I had returned.

'How are you now beta?' My mother said pulling my cheeks.

'Aur khaa lee pizza' My dad remarked as he looked at me.

'I am great' I said and kissed my mother on her cheek.

'I am sorry mom' A tear fell down my cheek.

'Its okay. Now don't cry. Punjabi boys don't cry!' She said and hugged me tightly.

I ate a little extra and slept a little extra too dreaming how my friends would react when I tell them the news!

Mothers are the only example of love at first sight because you fall in love with them the moment you enter this world and see them for the first time…

XI

'I finally have a girlfriend' I whispered to myself, maybe for the thousand and fifteenth time.

Yes! I finally had somebody to lean on!

The excitement didn't die the whole night.

I kept dreaming about silly things, like what probably could be our honeymoon destination, name of our kids and will she support me if I quit my job for writing?

'*Love nowadays isn't that eternal Mr Malhotra' a voice inside me spoke.*

It took me approximately one hour more than usual; to dress up for the school today. I didn't wanted to look like the old Sharief Malhotra.

The one who was the brand ambassador for Raksha Bandhan in his time. I wanted to look a little more appealing (though sexy will be the right word but I hate that word so I think we can settle on appealing).

I pressed the nozzle of the imported perfume thrice, later realising that it was a ladies perfume!

'Damn' I shouted angrily and put the perfume back on the table.

I went out of my room after taking another fifteen minutes to set my hair (I sense that you are laughing again. I am not to fault, love is).

I saw my father, mother and my ten years old sister sitting on the dining table. My father, staring in today's newspaper (maybe entertainment page) and my mother pouring corn flakes in my sister's bowl.

'Who sprayed my perfume?' My mother said, sniffing heavily the moment I sat on the dressing table.

I coughed, my sister offered me a glass of water and I drank whole of it.

'Looks like someone used the wrong perfume!' My mom said as I placed the glass back. My dad looked away from his newspaper, at me raising an eyebrow.

'Why so excited?' He said as his super sharp mind figured out that I used the wrong perfume in excitement.

How can parents be so omniscient?

'Who said I am excited' I said pouring some cereals in my bowl. I ate them and believe me, it was the best breakfast ever; though I ate these cereals from the past six years every morning but it was something about this morning.

I stood after having a few spoons.

'Bye Maa, bye dad!' I said touching their feet and leaving.

I heard a loud voice from upstairs.

'Idiot take your bag!' My father shouted. I just had opened the door of my car.

Damn, I wasn't to useless or dumb. What is she doing to me!

I ran upstairs and made a face, taking my bag with me and going back in the car.

Butterflies flew in my stomach. I looked at myself as a very lucky person to get a girl like Mahira. I smiled as the car rushed through the narrow roads. I didn't yell at my driver today when struck in traffic and skipped sad songs on my playlist.

'Thank you' I said as stepped out of the car. He smiled and then drove the car.

* * * *

I entered my class and everything seemed normal. I saw only my group mates in the room. It was a Saturday and only a few come school on a Saturday (from few I mean we).

I hugged my friends as I usually did and kept my bag on the table.

'Guys I have a little good news for you all' I said as all of them looked at me in surprise. I had told nobody about the 'yes'. Not even Utsav. I just wanted to see their reactions.

'You got pasta in your lunch box today' Priyanshu said as everyone burst into laughter.

'Fuck you Mishra' I said in disgust, 'Its even better.'

'Even better? Like a Pizza?' He said and again everyone burst into laughter like he was from the AIB.

I glared at them. It was above intolerable now. Utsav signalled me to keep calm.

'She said yes' I said it. My words were faster than Eminem's Rap God so it took a moment for my friends to figure out what I had said.

'She? Who Mahira? Like seriously' Utsav and Akshit said as Aryaman, that cute little bastard came near to hug me.

'Yes' I said as my group hooted and whistled and hugged me as if I just found out the cure for Ebola.

'We need party haan' Akshit said as he punched my stomach. Priyanshu's face was lit up with a huge smile, Aryaman and Utsav were happy too.

See, you always underestimate yourself. You are a good person!

'Taken things to hugs and kisses or not' Priyanshu said bringing his both folded hands closer to each other and producing sounds from mouth.

'I haven't even met her after yesterday! And mind it; I am not that kind of person' I said.

Yeah, I am not that kind of person even though I spend more than the annual budget for education, on tissue papers still am not that kind of person!

'Guys, I want to ask you one thing…' I said in a serious tone.

'Chocolate flavour will do it' Priyanshu said as at that very moment, I wanted to shoot a bullet through his head just like deadpool.

'…Am I a good person?' I spoke after a brief second.

I have a very bad habit of underestimating myself. Even though people laugh at my jokes, I think my jokes suck. Even though there are some people who are happy because of me, I think I am not a good person. I sometimes think I need to visit a Psychiatrist to get myself repaired!

'Bitch you are not a good person' Akshit said as I frowned.

See!

'But you are the best person!' He spoke hugging me tightly. So much tightly that I just skipped a breath or two. I literally broke into tears.

What else can one expect from life?

I kissed him on his cheek and returned him with a tighter hug.

Sometimes…. only friends are what we need!

'Leave emotional things…Tell me what you got in your lunch box?' Priyanshu said.

* * * *

I took a shower again (yes, shower two times with cold water in winters), dressed up and applied the *right* perfume this time. I saw myself in the mirror, getting ready for the tuition.

'What did she saw in you?' I asked looking in the mirror.

'Maybe something Mohini didn't saw!' Replied someone from inside.

I checked my watch, it was 3:00 of the evening. I had my tuitions at 4:30 so I still was left with plenty time. I decided to make a visit to the only stud I know hoping for some relationship advice; my cousin Gourav.

Gourav was five years elder than me. He had a good body physique, unlike me who looked like a blurred photo copy of R Madhavan. He was as tall as me, his muscles were more developed than my IQ and I looked at him as an ideal because he literally gave me the solution to every problem. One more fact, he was a stud. He banged and made new girlfriends faster than the time taken by the Dominos guy to deliver that pizza.

After 10 minutes of drive, I was there. Standing outside his house. His parents were working, he had two more sisters (which makes me wonder why they even bothered to buy a TV) but his sisters being a medical student, were always busy with studies or some work.

I knocked at the door. He opened it and looked at me with a smile. He wasn't wearing his T-Shirt and was probably flaunting his Abs.

'Sharief, my brother' he said, 'come in.'

I stepped inside and he locked the door from behind. I heard a female voice from upstairs.

'Gourav!' The voice shouted.

'Coming Jaan. Hey, lets go upstairs' he said and held my hand making me climb the stairs at the same pace as his.

As we reached, he opened the door and I found a beautiful (less beautiful than Mahira) girl sitting on the bed in a pink T-Shirt and jeans.

Who the hell is she and what the hell is she doing here?

'Sorry, I forgot an introduction. Sharief this is my girlfriend Risha and Risha this is my brother Sharief.' He said as I shook hands with her.

'But your girlfriend was…' I said remembering that he introduced me to someone else last week as he cut me in mid sentence

'My girlfriend was out of town but she is now in town. Sharief, you suffering from piles?' He said winking at me.

Piles? Me?

'No' I said.

'Then why don't you sit' he said in a cheap attempt to shift his girlfriend cum *sleep-with-me-once* cum *She-is-just-time pass's* mind away and guess what? He succeeded. His girlfriend laughed at it and I glared.

'Joking bro! Joking' he said and patted my back, 'so tell me why did you came here.'

I ensured that I sat on the chair and then said, 'I made a girlfriend.'

He literally clapped as Risha saw him in shock. Yes, something like 'Sharief Malhotra has a girlfriend' deserves a clap when heard for his brothers think he is gay due to lack of interest in girls.

'Finally! You did it!' He said and hugging me. It hurt me as his body build was Taylor Swift in comparison to mine.

'What's her name?' Risha said, with curiosity in her eyes.

'M…Mahira' I said and blushed. Even her name made me smile and grin like idiot for hours!

'That's hell nice of a name!' He said, 'but not better than Risha' he continued as he bent towards her and landed a kiss on her cheek. She murmured something like 'your brother is here' but still smiled and returned him with a kiss on his cheek. Have I told you earlier that even dogs making love sometimes turned me on? I probably have.

'So what are you waiting for? What do you want to ask?' He said looking at me.

'Am I good? Like good enough to be in a relationship with such a beautiful girl?' I asked him as a part of me told me I sucked and was the worst person who was ugly as fuck and didn't deserved something like that.

'You are so…cute and adorable! Why do you think you are not good?' She said and came forward to pull my cheek. I kind of hated when someone pulled my cheek, Utsav has a habit of doing it despite my warnings.

'You are hell lot of good guy! You'll kick some great ass's in relation I guess! It would be fun to see my brother, whom I thought was gay romancing with a girl! Its finally a dream come true' he said as I smiled.

'May I ask you one thing?' He said as I raised my eyebrow.

'Yes' I said.

'What's your size?' He said as my mind flew through dictionaries for the word 'size' in the context he said.

'Umm…Medium in tailored fit and large for a T-Shirt' I said as both of them burst into laughter.

'I know I am a little heavy but this doesn't means you'll laugh at me' I frowned.

'Not your shirt's size you idiot. Your…how should I put this…Your size!' He said as a huge library fell on my head and I understood what he meant.

Why the hell does he wants me to tell my size in front of his girlfriend? Just to flaunt that he got it bigger than me? And how can he expect me knowing my size? I have never seen Men in bathroom stalls holding scales to measure that!

'Its medium...Like medium' I said recalling from the memories of past 17 years and felt a little privacy invaded.

'Toti man! Medium toti man, I should say now!' He exclaimed and I was disgusted at him.

My cousins have a nude photo of me when I was maybe three or four. Every time I meet them, they shout 'Toti Man' and it kind of embarrasses me.

'Size doesn't matters. Do right things. Do good things. You surely deserve a girl' he said as the first part of his sentence reflected more irony than Rahul Gandhi but the later part made me feel a little better.

I glanced at the watch on the wall. It was 4:15. I stood up.

'Where?' He said rising from the bed.

'Tuitions' I said pointing to my bag.

'You didn't tell me how you met this girl' he said, looking at the roof maybe thinking 'you never told me!'

'Its a long story...Some other day' I said as I stood up. Yes, its a long story of how a pervert gets a girl even by wearing a cake laced jacket and stammering *please! Damn I regretted it every second of my life...*

I hugged Gourav and shook hands with Risha as I waved them good bye and sat in my car.

'Tuitions please' I said thinking.

Even though the story of my life sounds like it is straight out of 'Lolita', I loved my life and I loved Mahira too...

* * * *

I reached tuition. Believe me, if you were on Mahira's side, you would have broke up with me that day itself!

I don't know why but I behaved like a complete asshole. It looked like I was still not out of my *'hey she is my crush'* mode.

My mind ignored any sort of eye contact with her. I didn't even utter a single word. Others in the tuition had got the news from Utsav but were in doubt of it being true after observing my behaviour towards her.

She sat on the front desk while I sat two desks behind her. My beautiful view was blocked by Lady Hulk buster, Mansi. I kept leaning forward from time to time in order to get a view of her. Mansi noticed me.

'Am I blocking your view?' She said turning towards me.

'Yes' I said though it sounded rude but it was true. She stood up and addressed in air.

'Haan haan. Nobody needs their friends after coming in a relation! Oh god…save us from hypocrites!' She said. Though I knew she was joking like she always did, her words hurt me a little. I ignored her as she sat behind me and kept stabbing her pen in my back as a revenge.

The bell rang and I stood there, motionless, thinking what I had done.

'She should break up with you! You don't deserve her!' A voice inside me said and laughed.

I rushed downstairs and found her closing the door of her car. I couldn't help myself. Maybe this is the end. Like in Naayak, the protagonist becomes CM for a day what if I was a boyfriend for a day? As far as I know human behaviour, she can break up with me.

'Please god save me…Please!' I kept repeating in my head.

I took out my phone and texted her.

Sharief_Malhotra: **I am really very sorry for my behaviour today! I shouldn't have done that...I have issues making conversation with girls and making a conversation with the girl I love makes it even worse!**

She immediately saw the message and replied.

Mahi_bhatt_mb: **Awww...That's okay.**

A smile was lit on my face.

Mahi_bhatt_mb: **Why is there MB on your insta bio? It should be MS**

Sharief_Malhotra: **No No. MB means Mahira Bhatt Heart**

Her reply again made me smile, this time wider than before.

Mahira_bhatt_mb: **It should be MS. Mahira Sharief Heart**

I took her instructions and I changed my Insta's bio to 'M&S'

We later chatted endlessly until the car came to a screeching halt.

Sharief_Malhotra: **ILY Heart Good night love**

Mahi_bhatt_mb: **LY2 Heart Good night**

I knocked at the door and saw my dad standing there. I smiled at him. He looked a little angry and didn't smiled back.

'What happened?' I asked struggling for a straight face.

'We need to talk, Mr Malhotra' He said as I came inside the house.

XII

To be honest with you, I had got my balls in my mouth!

My dad sat next to me on the sofa. He was wearing his home clothes, kurta and pyjamas. He looked angry. With every passing second, I kept shitting bricks in my pant!

'*He will kill me!*' I mumbled to myself. He looked at me and raised an eyebrow.

'I don't think this is your age of doing this' he said and shook his head. He picked up the glass from the table and drank all of it in once. I looked for mom for only she was the one to save me from dad. She must be in her room, watching 'Aankhon se aasu episode-893'.

'What have I done?' I spoke to break the silence.

What have I done other than falling in love?

'What have you done? You read those kind of things and ask me what have you done?' He said more of shouted.

Read? What? Has he discovered an edition of 'Lolita' in my room? Or maybe 'Mastraam'? What if he has seen my internet history of 'Antarvasna.com'?

'Read what?' I said, my balls still in my mouth.

He didn't answered and just stood up and went to my room.

I sat there still, motionless and lifeless. I checked my pants if I took the phrase of 'Shitting bricks' literally. I hadn't.

He emerged exactly after five minutes back and sat on the sofa again holding a book in his hand. The moment I realised which book it was, I knew I was in trouble.

'Fifty shades of grey'

'Here, take your property back' he said as he threw it towards me. 'God I feel shame even holding it in my hand.'

You won't believe but I let out a laugh. I thanked god that he didn't find out that I had a girlfriend and a copy of 'Lolita' under my bed.

'You are laughing? You shameless creature!' He said as I shifted in the sofa.

'This is okay to read dad. Most of the people I know have read it. Its nothing…' I said in a convincing tone, 'In a University in the US, students were given a research task on this book to study 'Pop culture'. Its all due to modernisation.'

He looked in my eyes. His expressions melted and now he seemed to be cool. He looked down and was thinking something.

'Hai naa? I also think I over reacted. You are seventeen now. You have already read it anyways. I was just sitting in my office meeting when discussion of 'foreigners destroying Indian culture' came up and somebody raised the point of a book 'Fifty shades' being a bestseller even though containing graphic descriptions. It struck my mind at that moment that I had seen this novel in your room and I became angry' He said.

I smiled at him, my heartbeat now becoming somewhat 'normal'.

'How's life son?' he asked as he sat on the sofa again.

'Life's fine' I replied when I wanted to say *its god damn amazing!*

'Anything new?' he said. My parents probably suspected me being in a relationship.

You see, you can convince Indian parents that you have a girlfriend just by using Spray mint once, in front of them!

'Nothing new dad. Same old tuition, school and Rajma-Rice. I don't think there is something new' I said as I stood up to leave, 'good night dad.'

'Good night son and remember one thing. The people you get in your life are the one which you deserve. Had you not deserved them, they would have never came in your life. So take things easy' he said, his eyes gleaming like he knew each and everything on earth.

I nodded and went to my room. As I sat on my bed, his words kept repeating in my mind. I changed into my home clothes, removed my shoes and kept them aside.

You deserve her!

You deserve her!

You seriously deserve her!

To be honest, I probably am the last person you would fall in love with.

I have nothing special. Nothing. I am a superhero whose superpower is 'uselessness'. I am fat, ugly, I wear spectacles and much more.

So to remove some of the doubts from my mind, I took out a notebook from my bag and started to write my 'pros' and 'cons' on it.

Cons

1. Fat
2. Spectacles
3. Unusually low IQ
4. Ugly
5. Unusually low sense of humour
6. Fat (hey I mentioned this earlier)
7. Pervert

8. Grammar sucks
9. Bad person

Pros

1. I have money
2. I have a lot of novels

As you can see, there is nothing positive about me. I am that kind of person whose girlfriend will think thrice before introducing him to her friends. I stared at the page blankly.

'She will leave you… ' my idiotic side said.

'No she won't' the intelligent side cut him in mid sentence.

'What do you have? What special can you do? You are nothing but a 'below average' looking guy. A news like you have a girlfriend is more unbelievable than Asaram being a virgin!' The idiot said in a low, husky tone.

'Don't listen to him. I again say don't. He has fucking destroyed your life! You are a good person. You deserve her dude. Stop over thinking about it and get a break. You have to meet her tomorrow don't you' the intelligent guy said.

Maybe he was right. I was over thinking things. I crumbled the page and threw it to the other side of the room and slept.

Today was a Sunday but we had an extra class today in tuition. Though I am not much a person who would go for an 'extra class' and that too on 'Sunday', I woke up early, showered and changed into clean and ironed clothes.

'Bye dad bye mom!' I shouted outside their room as they were probably sleeping as they usually woke up late on Sunday mornings. I took my bag and looked for a last time (at least I called it the last time) in the mirror.

I sat in the car and said 'tuition'.

* * * *

I was greeted with fake smiles. At least I consider them fake. My eyes searched for Mahira but she hadn't arrived yet. Everyone smiled at me with a *we-know-everything-about-you* look. I ignored everyone's smiles as at that moment, a girl came through the door wearing the 'smile' I had wanted.

Mahira was there, dressed in a blue half jacket on a red T-shirt and blue jeans.

She. Looked. Beautiful.

She waved her hand at me and I waved my hand back. I kept staring her and I think she noticed. Damn!

I had told her so many times that she was the most beautiful girl in the world. Yet, the stubborn she was she never found my words true. I praised her endlessly. Like more praised than BJP workers ever did of Modi ji. She meant the world to me. Her simplicity was the only thing that made me fall in love with her again and again but every time I told her my feelings, she said 'There is nothing like that. I am not that beautiful. No I am not. Haha!'

I think underestimating themselves is the biggest talent the female gender has got. They will apply tons of makeup (Mahira never did useless makeup so mind your tongue before speaking about her), will wear expensive clothes, travel in big cars, get their HD pictures clicked by their friend zoned friend who got a DSLR and still at the end of the day will feel like they are the most 'ugly' and not the most 'beautiful'.

Dear females, if you want to see what 'Ugly' really means kindly give me your e-mail. I will send you a picture of mine and then I don't think you will call yourself ugly ever!

She sat on one of the front desk, me being four desks (which felt like four continents) behind her and started chatting with her friends. At that moment, Isha her long time (since third I guess) best friend arrived but she ignored her and Isha too rolled her eyes. She sat with Karan, her boyfriend. The guy who thinks he is the most handsome boy in the universe and has fucked maybe half of the entire human race till now (the latter being true).

'Hey, all good?' I asked Isha as Karan looked at me with a cheerful smile. I sometimes thought he was gay for he texted me 'baby I love you' one night.

'All good? Nothing is good! It's over! All over' she kind of shouted in a painful tone turning towards me.

'I think you can tell me. Maybe I can help you' said the guy who can't even change an infant's diaper.

'I told you. It's all over. Me and Mahira are not friends anymore. People change after coming into relationship' she said and rolled her eyes at me.

'You want to tell me or not. I can help you, I assure' I said as I took out my phone and started playing 'GTA Vice city' (which I had illegally downloaded yesterday) on it.

'Okay so listen. She didn't tell me that you two are in relation! I mean she hid it from me! She was the first person to get the news that me and Karan are in relation. Poor me' she said in an anger and pain mixed tone.

'And?' I said.

'You listening?' She said as I locked my phone and kept it on the desk.

'My friends from the old school keep telling me that you have changed after coming into a relation. Even Mahira says that. I mean how can they say that? You yourself see that I hardly spend fifteen minutes out of the three hours with Karan. What about the rest two hour forty five minutes? I tell you, she is not the same Mahira' she said with the ultimate weapon that is worse than a nuclear bomb: a girl's tear, ready to shoot from her eyes.

'You won't believe that I asked her if she will agree to come in a relation with when you proposed her on your birthday. She said she won't and I hear this after some days!'

'You see, you don't simply end friendships or relationships when there is some communication gap. Both of you need to talk to each other. I read it somewhere that "When nails grow, you cut the nails not the fingers. Just like that, when ego grows you cut the ego not the friendship". You both are mature enough to sort this out. She also must be at fault but you need to do this by yourself' I said, a little proud of my monologue.

One will never believe that these words have been spoken by the same guy who fears from peeing in night, when there is no light.

'She's your girlfriend. You will take her side. You are not being unbiased. Your words are influenced by her' she said as she turned forward again.

I felt bad for her. Yes, I had heard that she had changed but I never observed it. For me, Isha was the same girl whom I told that I loved Mahira for the first time. I scratched my head. There can be something I can do to save their friendship. The chemistry sir came at that very instant and started to teach.

'And one more thing. She lied to me once. That she was in relation with a guy. I won't tell you his name, but she lied. She isn't my friend anymore' she turned towards me again and sobbed, loud enough for the teacher to hear it.

'Isha and Sharief. If there is some problem please discuss it afterward's. Let's study for now' the teacher said as he started teaching.

I don't know why but I tore a little slip from the back page of my notebook and wrote 'I Love you. Now smile please :)' on it and told Ayesha to pass it to Mahira. There was a constant risk that the chit might be caught but the brave person I was (not enough brave to go to pee alone at night), I took my chances.

In five seconds the chit reached her. She read it and turned towards me and smiled. A smile that was enough for me to forget how ugly, screwed up or fucked up I was. A wide idiotic grin appeared on my face as she turned forward again.

Exactly after one hour and thirty two minutes, the bell rang. It was recess time.

'Any plans on going to a date?' Utsav asked me, looking like one of the gay characters from Sajid Khan movies for he trimmed his beard.

'Yes' I said and stood up. I went to Mahira.

'Let's go to the NesCafe' I said as she nodded and stood up.

'Can we also go. Please. Please. Pretty please' Mansi said as I recalled that I had only two hundred bucks and nodded.

We walked through the corridor, didn't uttering a single word. I told her that we could go by the lift and we stood there, for the lift to arrive. The rest of the girls had made their way through stairs.

The lift arrived and I signalled her to enter it first, like a gentleman. I entered the lift too and pressed the 'Ground' floor.

The moment the lift started to move, the song 'Crazy in love' from the movie fifty shades of grey started to play loudly in my head. The lift scene of the movie came in my mind. I felt a little awkward.

Is this the right time?

From one eye I peeked at the CCTV. It was facing towards us.

Got me looking so crazy right now your love has got me looking so crazy right now

Got me looking so crazy right now your kiss got me looking so crazy right now

I thought of the possibilities of a failed attempt to kiss. They were:

1. Getting slapped
2. Appearing in the newspaper with 'Pervert teen forces himself on an innocent girl'
3. Getting thrown out of the institute.

I clenched my teeth and dismantled that useless, pervert idea. I couldn't take any chances. The lift stopped on the second floor.

'Mansi, I tell you' she said and let out a laugh. I shook my head and smiled.

'Mahira, I love you' I said in the same tone I had said on my birthday. Stammering, stuttering and fearing tone. It looked like I was never going to come out of *hey-she-is-my-crush* mode.

'I love you too' she said and my head went tizzy.

Wow! Someone loves me! I am ugly as fuck but still someone loves me!

'I am a little mentally retarded na?' I said as she shook her head.

'No you are not' she smiled.

It took three minutes for the fifteen second journey in the lift for Mansi had clicked each and every button of each floor. The lift opened as I again let her leave first.

'Did you do something?' Mansi said laughing and giggling with the other girls.

'Not everyone is like you Mansi' Mahira said and rolled her eyes. She laughed again and I was kind of disgusted at her absurd laughter.

I took two kit kats (some 'sense' one which is more expensive and sweet than the regular one) and gave them to Mahira. I handed the remaining hundred bucks to Mansi later wondering I didn't even spent a penny on myself. She told me to buy a burger for her.

'Do you want to vomit?' The guy on the counter said in a heavy fake accent.

'What? Why would I want to vomit?' I asked puzzled.

'Do you want vomit?' He again said in broken English. He was probably testing his English on me.

'I don't understand. Why would I want to vomit? I am well' I said. He shook his head.

'Arrey garam karna hai?' (Do you want to warm it?)

I nodded in horror and went to take a seat.

I played Grand Theft Auto on my phone as Mahira talked to her friends. I sat on a chair which was a little away from their chairs. I had no interest in eaves dropping on female conversation.

After ten minutes I stood up.

'We should go now' I said as everyone stood up and we left the Cafe.

'What did Isha told you?' Mahira asked with curiosity in her eyes.

'Nothing. She just said that she is angry and sad that you didn't tell her about our relation and that you think she has changed' I said.

'She has changed no?' She asked me. Being a good boyfriend, I nodded.

'You won't believe how hard she slammed the door yesterday when she left the car after I told her about us. Even my brother was like 'what the!' She said and we laughed.

'Please sort it out with her. Everything. Don't let the friendship be broken because of silly reasons. People will tomorrow say that even you changed after coming in a relation and I don't want this to happen' I said as we entered the lift.

Only we were in the lift again. I smiled and pressed the 'Third floor'.

XIII

'Bye Sharief' she said and waved her hand at me as the class ended.

'Bye!' I said and smiled. She started to walk with her group of friends who were more random in nature than the motion of gaseous particles!

Utsav came from behind and slapped my back.

'Bitch gets a girlfriend and forgets his brother!' He said and laughed.

He was kind of wrong. I didn't change myself. The person who had changed was him. He used to call me every day, talk for maybe half an hour discussing the least important things possible and laughed at each other's shitty jokes. The day he came into a relation, he kind of forgot us all. He barely called once a week, kept himself busy with his girlfriend and was stuck on phone all the time even when he was hanging out with us.

These things didn't hurt much but what did hurt me the most was that he now shared his lunch box with his girlfriend!

'Nah. I can never forget my friends' I said and smiled. Yes, friendship day can never replace valentines.

'What's the plan for today?' He said as we got out of the main building.

'Mom and dad want me to go to some family function. Cousin's engagement' I said and frowned. Its not about attending a family function but trust me, at the end of the day your back seriously hurts after touching feet of the most random people around!

'Enjoy' He said and smiled.

'You got any plans for today?' I asked as the driver opened my car's door.

'No plans until FAN releases! Few weeks and there we are, my birthday!' He said as I waved a middle finger on his face.

He and his Shah Rukh fever!

The driver drove slowly through the small lanes which could have been mistaken as Ants going on work from the sky provided the level of traffic. Cars honked, people cursed and spat on the roads blaming the Indian government for all this. I picked up the remote from the adjacent seat, skipped to a romantic track and increased the volume of the music player.

'Sir you look happy' the driver said as he looked in the rear view mirror. I smiled at him.

'Happy birthday bhaiya' I said as it suddenly hit me that it was his birthday today.

'Thank you sir. Thank you so very much' he said and gleamed, 'Sir and mam had already wished me in the morning.'

'Why do I look happy to you bhaiya?' I asked with curiosity exploding in every part of my mind.

Is it that simple to sense someone's happiness?

'I am sorry sir. I shouldn't have said that' he said, expressionless probably thinking that I was hurt by his comment.

'No bhaiya. You shouldn't be sorry. Just tell me why do I look happy, please' I said extending the 'please' to a much larger extent. He laughed.

'You don't curse me for traffic. You keep smiling, have lost the concept of 'time'. I have never seen you this happy sir. Congratulations for whatever the reason is' he said. I smiled. There was something very Batman-Alfred about me and him. He was our driver from the past five years.

'Thank you bhaiya! So what's the plan? You should have been on a holiday today. I could have taken an auto. Why spoil your day?' I asked.

'I am going back home after I drop you, sir and mam to the function. My family is already so much excited. I had told them I will order a pizza for them this evening.'

'Then hurry up please' I said patting his shoulder as he stepped his feet on the accelerator.

* * * *

'Sharief! Hurry up! What do you want your Seema massi to say? Her cousin sister was late and wasn't able to catch his son's engagement? Jaldi kar (Hurry up)' my mother said as she wore her earings and adjusted herself in the mirror. She looked really beautiful, like always.

I went in my room and scanned it. Socks, books, T-shirts and jeans were all I was able to see. I picked up a blue coloured T-shirt and wore it with a black jacket. I looked in the mirror.

Average. 1/10 in looks.

I shook my head and got out of my room. I saw my dad staring the mirror which was expected never to happen before the world ends!

One silly function and the whole family becomes conscious of their looks!

'The driver's waiting. Its his birthday. Go and sit in the car' he said. I nodded and started to walk downstairs.

My mother came running behind me.

'Sharief! Sharief!' she said as I stopped in the stairs. She came near me and applied a little black tikka behind my ear and pulled my cheeks hard. I wanted to tell her that there are maybe a million guys outside in the whole world who are zillion times good looking and smarter than me. *Mothers, they never change.*

I sat in the car and waited for my well dressed family to come down. Once everyone was in the car, the driver ignited the engine.

'Bhaiya is going like this? in these clothes?' my little sister said.

'Yes' I nodded.

In seventeen minutes we were there. KC Residency. One of the costliest hall in the city. From costly halls to clothes, Punjabi's love to show off. I got out and excused myself from my family for a second to spray mouth freshener in my mouth. After four sprays, I returned back.

'You sure he doesn't smokes?' my father asked to my mother. I rolled my eyes.

We entered the hall in the ground floor. I saw some of the people for the first time. People were dressed like it was a fashion competition! Random women pulling my cheeks, random uncles slapping my stomach and saying *'Patla ho gaya hai'* (Lost quite some weight) and touching feet of infinite people is way too much.

My parents sat on a chair. Waiter served them with spring rolls and paneer tikkas which they placed on a tissue paper and put it on the circular table next to them slowly eating using a tooth pick. Smiles were being exchanged with the most random people. Sounds of laughing emerged from some part of the room. The stage was empty as both, the boy and the girl were busy in doing there fake makeup. Kids hooted like they were from a zoo. Alcohol was being served and believe me, no table was empty without a glass filled with it!

'Didi! Didi' I saw a women running towards my mother. I recognised her. She was Sweety massi, from Jalandhar. I touched her feet and she sat on a chair near my mom.

'Sweety!' my mom hugged her as if they were meeting after fourteen years when; in reality it was just three months.

'Didi has he got Asthma?' she said looking at me with a serious expression.

I was shocked.

Asthma? Me? Why?

'No…N…No. Who told you' my mother said equally shocked, stammering.

'I saw him spraying something in his mouth, outside' she said as it suddenly hit me that she was talking about the mouth freshener.

Damnnnnn! Asthma spray and mouth freshener are two different things. Damnnnn!!!

I wanted to shout but laughed inside. A laugh horrible enough for all the heads to turn to me.

'Massi. It is mouth freshener not Asthma pump' I said and sat next to her laughing hard.

She probably didn't have the concept of a mouth freshener and made a face. I took out my phone and checked if Mahira was online. I refreshed it thrice. She wasn't. I missed her already.

I felt a pat on my shoulder. I turned back to see Gourav, the hunk dressed in a white shirt and blue jeans which could easily melt the hell out of any girl's heart. He surely looked like a Greek god, his shirt finding it difficult to cover his muscles. I smiled the moment I saw him.

He came to my parents and touched their feet. They blessed him.

'Can I go with Gourav bhai?' I asked them as both of them nodded simultaneously. I stood and followed him through brilliantly dressed people. I mentally kicked myself for looking so much average.

We sat in a corner. I fished out my phone again to check if she was still online. I refreshed the feed fifteen times. Again, she wasn't.

'How are you Mr Malhotra? How is the relation going? Your first girlfriend' he said and giggled. Okay, she was my first girlfriend but I don't think there is something to laugh in it.

'She's fine. How is your girlfriend?' I asked in a proud tone.

Take it in the face, I also have a girlfriend!

'She's fine. Want a drink?' he said as I shook my head. He stood up and was back with a glass of beer and a glass of cold drink, the latter one for me of course.

'I want you to tell me how this started' he said with curiosity in his eyes like in a kid's. He looked cute as well as hot at the same time. Something I wasn't capable of looking even if taken one at a time!

In the next half hour, I narrated him all the events of my past six months to him. He listened to me like a kid listens to his father, questioning me on points he didn't got. I told him everything from the start. The story of a shy gayish guy getting a girlfriend can make a bestseller, I told to myself.

'THIS IS FUCKING AMAZING!' he shouted and banged his fist on the table. 'My brother is so much fucking romantic, I never knew that! God!'

'Easy' I said, 'Don't shout' I whispered to him, sipping from my glass of cold drink.

'You know what, I have a friend. He is a *struggling* writer. Only a few know him. He is trying to write a novel since two years but hasn't succeeded in it. This can be a kickass story if I tell him this. Its far better than what he is writing right now, 'The Man who had everything'. He will be happy' he said as I raised my eyebrow.

'You think?' I asked puzzled.

'Of course' he said and squeezed my shoulder, 'Shayaries haan'. I smiled.

He stood up.

'Got to leave brother. Sorry but Risha has her college fest today. She is performing in it. I didn't wanted to miss it and now after hearing your story, I can't miss it!' he said, 'Want to come with me?'

'No. I will be fine here' I shook my head and hugged him. He always hugged me tightly. So tightly that I might be having an internal injury because of his hugs!

I fished my phone out again and refreshed the feed thirty three times. No message from anyone and she still wasn't online.

Is everything okay? Why isn't she online?

I typed a message.

Sharief_Malhotra: **Where are you? No messages today? All okay? Missing your beautiful messages. Love you.**

I pressed the send button and looked around. Plenty of time was still left for the ceremony to start. I didn't wanted to indulge myself with my Punjabi relatives again. I stood up and placed some of the tandoori chicken in my plate and took another glass of cold drink and sat again on the same chair. I placed my plate carefully on the table because it was probably overloaded. I started having bits of chicken with the cold drink while I thought about my early ages of life.

When I was ten

I was the kid whom you hated the most. The most nerdy idiot in the class. The one who reminds the teacher about the home work when the whole class hadn't done it. Girls were like alien to me. All my other friends talked to girls but I didn't. I rather solved maths questions and learn EVS than talking to girls. The only view I had towards girls was that they were my competitors. Every year I saw the name of a girl being scribbled on the top of the blackboard while my name just behind next to it. I came second and it burnt me. Girls, in my opinion were a weapon of mass destruction as well as distraction. I was kind of cute that time. Girls from the senior classes pulled my cheeks and it gave me a tingling sensation down my spine. They would sometime take me to their class and show me to their friends. "Aw…So cute baby" they would say and I wouldn't react, keeping the only thing of coming first in my mind.

When I was twelve

Reproduction was the newest thing in our ears. Until I was twelve, I thought that people pray to god and god gives them children on the basis of their deeds. My friends would fantasise about women. They thought women were the only thing that had to be discussed and to be kept talking about the whole day. Some of my friends ended up being in a relationship.

"Puppy love bullshit" I would say and dismissed their thoughts of being in love and time going into slow motion but deep down, I burnt. I burnt with jealousy. By now, I had made a few girl-friends. Mohini Sharma was one of them. Her seat was assigned with me and we sat together, discussed things and studied together. Her roll number was just next to me so we sat nearby in the exam halls cheating whatever was possible. I wasn't in love with her. I was just attracted. Attraction, that it.

When I was thirteen

The thirteenth year was one of the worse and one of the best year of my life at the same time. I had discovered something that everybody does to maybe get stress free. I won't take the name but yes, everybody does that.

My friends discussed that with me. There was a very tragic incident based on lies and rumours in my life that time. Though, I am completely over it right now it had made me go fucking insane. I had cut my wrists, tried to jump from the roof and was a total mental torture. My grades were fucked up. I got straight 'D' and 'E' grades but thanks heaven they don't fail students in sixth grade so my ass was safe. I got over that thing in that year itself. Studies didn't bothered me anymore. I turned into a guy who secretly fantasised for every women. I struggled to keep a clean image of myself in the mind of my class mates in which I succeeded. Discussions on Maths and Science were replaced by 'Size' now. Every guy in the class wanted to know each other's size. Though I never told them mine, deep down I knew I was lagging.

I googled everything on it. Size increase exercises didn't worked out for me. I was struck with a medium size when I wanted it to be large. I wanted it to be feared. I wanted it to be more feared than Osama Bin Laden! Once I knew I had to live with it, I accepted whatever it was and moved on in life.

When I was fourteen

God's natural way of keeping teenagers single! Yes, I am talking about 'pimples' stuck me. They were all over my face. My hormones raged. I was secretly in love with Mohini, which I never told her because I didn't wanted our friendship to end because honestly, I knew she deserved a much better boy. The one with less pimples, taller than me and the one with an extraordinary size! The boy I wanted to become once.

I dabbed my face with toothpastes, face washes, face packs whatever was available at home. I heard other people say that you get pimples when you do that...um...er...stress releasing exercise. I stopped doing that and voila, pimples fucked my face even worse! By the end of the fourteenth year, I had managed to get a clean face and the only thing that now stressed me out was my 'height'.

All these commercials on TV are fake! I repeat, fake! I bought almost all the dietary supplements from the market which promised me a growth in my height. I drank them everyday, thrice or more times on some days wishing I would grow just like the 'beanstalk' from 'Jack and the bean stalk' story.

I hanged for hours until I felt I was like one of those characters from 'Fantastic Four' with long arms. I wished only one thing, to be tall and less fat. I worked on my looks and tried to improve them making me a little average looking which was better than the earlier *tribal looking idiot!*

I wanted to become desirable for women though I didn't repeated my old mistake this time. I excelled at studies at the same time while looking more manly and handsome.

Tight shirts, pants hanging low and expensive underwear's didn't work for me. They made me look like a tard instead of a 'Greek God'. Till I reached mid fifteen, I had accepted myself and cursed myself daily for the average looks god had given me.

My chain of thoughts were broken by my mom's words. I saw her standing still, looking at me as I put the leg bone of the chicken down.

'Its about to start! Its about to start. Lets go' she said as I stood up and walked near the stage. The bride appeared from the right as I saw some boys, which were probably her ex.'s or maybe friend zoned clapping and whistling. The groom appeared from the right, dressed in a well fitted suit. Ankit, was one of two kids my Seema massi had. He looked handsome and I clapped.

Both of them took the stage and he put a ring, which was of two lakh thirty five thousand (Abracadabra! Its not magically I know its price. Being in a Punjabi family, such things are the topic of our discussion) around her finger and she blushed. Maybe she too knew the market price of the ring. I clapped and imagined me and Mahira in that place. She would look beautiful in that dress, I told myself.

'Only five varieties of chicken! The girl side is giving a Safari in dowry and see, how mean the boy side is! Just five varieties!

We had seven in Priya's wedding when the boy side was gifted with a Wagon R. Damn! Kitna kam kharcha kiya hai' I heard someone say.

'Eat before it gets over. I heard its limited, per plate system' the person next to me said in thin air probably to me and the crowd started to walk towards the food counters as the Bride and Groom got their useless photographs in forced poses clicked.

XIV

I open my eyes. It's all dark.

I try to move my hands but feel like they are chained to the roof. My arms hurt and so does my wrist. The sound of chains makes it even worse. I am tired as hell and my mouth craves for water.

I can't see anything!

'Where am I?' I shout hoping someone would listen.

No reply.

My voice echoed and this made me guess I was in a large room.

What am I doing here?, I ask myself.

I repeat the past memories. I was in my cousin's engagement ceremony in a large hall which was brightly lighted full of well dressed people. Then how come am I here? A room that is so dark that it could even put batman's cave to shame. A place where my arms are chained to the roof. A place where my own voice echoes.

Is this Fifty Shades of Grey?

'Hello! Is anybody there?' I shout again. Suddenly I hear screeching of tires. My heartbeat became abnormal.

Just thirty seconds after the screeching of tires being heard, I heard a door bang open in the other corner of the room. As the door opened, little light entered the room and I could see a person who was less heightened than me standing. The shadow moved towards me and I heard a click. The lights came on and blurred my vision.

As my iris adjusted back, I saw the person and recognised him immediately.

He was Mahira's brother!

He was wearing a red T-Shirt and an evil smile on his face. His beard complemented his evil smile and I think I shit in my pants.

'What am I doing here?' I ask him. He didn't respond and raised an eyebrow.

'What are you doing here? You are asking me? Ask yourself!' he shouted and then spat on the floor.

'Is it because your sister is my um…er…girlfriend?' I barely managed to speak in a combined state of fear and thirst. Maybe her brother was a sadist!

'Congrats! You win fifty million rupees for the correct answer! Who do you think you are huh?' he said as I tried to move my arms again but nothing happened.

'I am sorry for all this. I am really sorry. Please remove this chain, its hurting me' I said as he looked away.

'Sir, I am really sorry. But I think that even you have a girlfriend so as per logic, even she's someone's sister. Why are you torturing me here? Ain't we all equal? in love?' I continued hoping he would let me go.

'People think thrice before even taking my name. And you? fell in love with my sister? Believe it my boy, its the worst mistake of your life and probably the last too' He said as he went outside the room.

I scanned the room. It was all red coloured with the roof being painted brown. I never thought I would end my crappy yet happy life here, in a red coloured room being tortured till death by my girlfriend's brother!

He returned back with a suitcase. He opened it and what I saw was horrible! He had a torture kit!

'Sorry sir! I am sorry! Please' I said as he ignored all my humanitarian appeals and took out something that looked like a screw driver.

'You might have heard about I-SIS son but I-BRO is much fucking worse!' he said, laughing on his own joke and inserting that screw driver right into my leg slowly…

'WHAT THE F…!' I shout as I wake up with a jerk in my car. I see my sister sitting in my father's lap in the seat adjacent to my driver as the driver continued to drive.

My vision focuses to my mother who was sitting just next to me.

'What happened beta?' my mother said placing her hand on my face. My father turned back to me.

'All okay?' he said.

'Yes, yes' I said and both of them nodded.

Shit! That was hell lot of a nightmare. Is this a possibility? or in her words, is this an option? Mahira's brother torturing me to death? I think he surely will if he finds out the truth.

I wiped the sweat beads off my face and opened the window.

'Where are we going?' I ask as my father again turned back towards me.

'Home. Where else you idiot!' he said in a loud tone and I regretted asking that question. I looked away.

'You sure he doesn't takes drugs too?' My father asked my mother.

* * * *

The moment I entered my room, I fished out my phone which was out of battery probably because of refreshing the Instagram feed for three hundred and fifty times and maybe because of the three hour long 'Temple Run' session too.

I inserted the charge plug and fired it to power.

Without wasting any second, I opened my Instagram and saw her message there.

Mahi_bhatt_mb: **Sorry but actually I had gone to Isha's home to sort everything out. She got no WiFi there so I wasn't able to receive or reply to your texts…**

A wide smile of relief that she was okay spread on my face.

Sharief_Malhotra: **Everything sorted out with her now? That's hell lot of a good news!**

Mahi_bhatt_mb: **Yes!!!**

I felt a little tired from the useless family function and the dreadful nightmare I had just witnessed so I texted her a Good night.

Sharief_Malhotra: **Good night <3 I Love you**

Mahi_bhatt_mb: **I love you too…Good night!**

I yawned and jumped on my bed. No nightmare can disturb your sleep when you know there is someone though a little far away from you, who loves you!

I got up early and did some push ups. From some, I mean ten. I took a shower, applied some nice perfume and got ready for the school. I tried to act as normal as possible in front of my parents for they already think I have a girlfriend.

As I walked through the corridor, I heard some random voices of students whispering in each other's ears.

'Even he has girlfriend! Haha! What did she see in him?' One boy whispered to the other.

'Don't know. I thought he was a fucking gay who had no interest in girls. Oh god! we the one's with a dick are single and dickless guys are getting girlfriend!' The other said and let out a breath.

I wanted to smash his fucking ugly face but restrained myself. I entered the class and saw everyone seated.

'Now when people are in a relation, they forget their friends. They change. Huhuhu' Akshit fake cried mocking me with his satirical comments. I rolled my eyes at him.

'He hasn't changed. He is still the same Sharief Malhotra. Stop doing it to him bro' Aryaman said as he looked even more cute with his new haircut.

'Fuck you doobs! You think I am serious? Our brother never changed and he never will' he said taking out a portable comb from his coat's pocket and hugging me while combing his hair, showing a perfect example of 'Multi tasking'.

I saw Utsav enter the class with his girlfriend, Ayesha. Both of them holding hands like a mother-son afraid to be lost in the carnival.

'Hello friends' Utsav said as he was greeted with middle fingers and eye glares for he brought his girlfriend in the class.

You see, this is where it all starts. Why does he have to bring his girlfriend in our class? Why does he have to make our group formal in front of her? Nobody can talk when she arrives because whatever we talk about, is surely not suitable for a women to hear.

Can you discuss how many times you did that er.... stress releasing exercise yesterday, in front of your friend's girlfriend? can you discuss the name of the last porn you saw? or can you discuss 'cleavages'?' Probably not. The main problem with Utsav sometimes is that he gets carried away.

She's in our tuition and she's in our school too. I don't think there will be an issue if he excuses himself from her just for the school time and later does whatever he wants to in the tuition. Ayesha is my friend since sixth standard and she kind of knows all my ups and downs. Still there is a gender thing that differences the two ideologies (though I know girl's talk the same bullshit as boys do but behave like they were thrown from the heaven on earth with no idea of anything).

'Okay, we can go outside' he said as he took her outside the class.

'Why does he even brings her in here? Doesn't he knows I get turned on even by seeing good food let alone the thing of seeing a girl?' Priyanshu said as all of us burst into laughter.

'So how's everything going?' He asked as I sat next to him.

'Its going fine. Smooth and slow' I said as Aryaman giggled.

'Kissed?' Priyanshu said.

'Not yet' I said. *Is it necessary to kiss in a relationship?*

'This guy hasn't even held her hand and you expect him to kiss her?' Akshit said and laughed.

Priyanshu's face became serious. Like he was thinking something. Something big.

'Operation Hold Hands' he announced proudly, 'starts today.'

Everyone clapped as I scratched my head unaware of what was going around.

'Is it necessary to do so? Hold her hand?' I said. *Love can work without touch too my friend.*

'Of course it is. You need to show that you care for her. I googled 'What does holding hands means in a relationship' and the results were astounding! The website said that holding hands can reduce stress, increase the bond and even helps better understanding of the two' He said as I laughed. When people like me use Google to search bestsellers, my friend searched 'What does holding hand means in a relationship'.

'So how would I do that?' I ask out of context feeling totally alien.

'You got to do nothing. Just offer her your hand. Like just move your hand towards her and she'll hold it. That's it. Simple as hell' he said as everyone nodded and Utsav entered the class again, this time alone and sat in front of me.

'What if she ends up giving a high five to me?' I asked, imagining the scenario which would fit in any Rom-Com.

He laughed with his expressions still serious.

'She won't. Girl's love when their boyfriend expresses himself as a typical caretaker for them. The things you do, chat and write shayaries can be even done when friends. What is the main purpose of a relationship then?' he said as I nodded.

He was kind of right.

'Okay. So I am in' I said as all the other members of our so called *justice league* clapped like I agreed to go to Syria and shoot each and every ISIS member down single handed.

'One more thing. Stop spamming our group on Instagram with messages on her! "She looks so beautiful in her new photo", "oh my god, look at her. She's so pretty" and "Her new DP made me fall in love with her again". Keep this shit to yourself. Why do you do so? to jealous us?' he said as I raised an eyebrow.

'Why would I need to jealous you? You are my brothers, right? Its all because I am madly in love with her. Trust me, madly' I said and everyone laughed except Utsav. Maybe only he understood my situation for he was like the one of the two Asaram clones in a thousand virgins of our group!

'Take all this love up your ass and tell me, what have you got in the lunchbox! I will surely rape you if its paneer again' he said as the teacher entered at that moment and the school started, like it always does.

It was our games period and we were playing a girls vs boys cricket match. I, being a good bowler was made to bowl five complete overs. I took four wickets, Mohini Sharma being one of them.

She didn't reacted like she earlier did. I heard her boyfriend or whatever he was for her, broke up with her. She faced disgusting comments. She went through a bad time. I wanted to tell her that being a good friend, I was always there for her but never did.

Tired and exhausted I sat on the side of the ground alone. Unexpected, I felt someone just sat next to me. Mohini!

'How's life Sharief?' she asked me. I remembered that once I had asked her how's life, she replied 'He's fine'. Its the time for a revenge.

'She's fine' I said with a forced smile.

'Miss Mahira, the girl of your dreams haan? Forgot me so early? Never expected this' she said looking down on the ground.

I saw her face. She had became quite weak and looked tired with dark circles under her eyes which symbolised her lack of sleep.

'Yes. I love her' I said as proudly as possible.

'Love. It makes us go insane' she said and laughed. We were talking like this after a year.

'Hey, I read that Half Girlfriend. Damn sexy book' she said as I nodded, 'thank you.'

'Your welcome' I said and stood up.

'Leaving your old friend behind, alone?' she said with her blue eyes glittering again.

'Friends? Something we never were. Bye' I walked away from the field.

* * * *

I reached my home and changed into black shirt and blue jeans.

Why does Mohini wants us to be friends again?

Is she jealous?

Does she miss me?

I shook my head as I had much important things to focus instead, Mission holding hands being one of them. So here was my plan:

I would be talking to her like I always do and then suddenly move my hand towards her, without any suspicion. Then I would hold her hand and tell her that I really love her.

This shit looks really filmy when thought about. I expect some background music after the operation is successful. I prayed to god for not making the fate of 'Operation hold hands' as same as 'Operation Mid night call'.

Looking a little better after trimming my beard, I got out of the house and sat in the car.

I smiled as the driver looked at me from the rear view mirror.

'Tuition' I said as I fished out my phone.

Sharief_malhotra: **How was your day?**

Mahi_bhatt_mb: **It was amazing as well as tiring!**

Sharief_Malhotra: **What was amazing about it?**

Mahi_bhatt_mb: **Everything!!!**

She looked happy. Maybe it was because of Isha and her patching up again.

Sharief_Malhotra: **Had lunch?**

Mahi_bhatt_mb: **Yes. You?**

Sharief_Malhotra: **Yes. See you in the tuition. Bye.**

Mahi_bhatt_mb: **Bye!!**

I switched my phone off and kept it in my bag, my stomach full of butterflies for 'Operation Hold hands'.

Fifteen minutes of speeding through tight lanes and heavy traffic, I was there. As the car stopped near the main building, I got out of it and signalled my driver to leave.

I entered the main building and pressed the button to call the elevator. Thirty seconds later, the elevator arrived and I was in it.

It travelled at terminal velocity. My heart thumped from the thoughts of what a successful 'Operation hold hands can lead to'. The lift stopped at third floor and I got out of it.

I entered the class, when the chemistry teacher was already teaching some organic chemistry on the blackboard. I mentally kicked myself for waving a hand at Mahira before wishing the teacher 'Good evening'. He rolled his eyes at me.

'As late as always' He said as Mahira smiled.

'Sorry sir' I sat on my seat next to Utsav.

'The next question will be answered by Sharief Malhotra' the teacher said as he turned towards the blackboard and started writing something. I looked at Mahira with my expressions dull. I couldn't answer any question of chemistry! She gave me a *its-okay-you'll-surely-answer-that-right* look. I smiled at her.

'Okay so Sharief, tell me the organic name of this chain compound' he said as he pointed to a 'M' drawn on the blackboard.

The whole class burst into laughter. Even Mahira. My head went tizzy. Was it his sarcastic way of telling me that he knew everything?

Yes, I had a very bad history with the letter 'M'. Mohini's name started from 'M' and so does Mahira's. My friends kept calling me 'M' man. I frequently liked people whose name started from a 'M'. It was an 'M'azing feeling. Yes, Aap Sharief ke peeche aur Sharief 'M' ke peeche, too much fun.

'That's Pentane sir' Mahira answered out of context, breaking my chain of heavy thoughts.

'Okay. So from now onwards, we are going to call Mahira as Sharief, right class?' he said raising an eyebrow as the whole class again burst into laughter.

Chemistry sucks but a person in love sucks even more!

After a thousand glances at Mahira and three hours, the bell rang.

Operation hold hands!

I stood up and went to Mahira. She looked extremely beautiful in her grey jacket. Just like my girl.

'We could go for a walk behind the building' I said as she smiled and nodded. Isha and Karan followed us too downstairs.

'I got a very bad dream yesterday' I told her. Her expressions turned serious.

'What happened?' she asked.

'Your brother tortures me' I said and both of us laughed. Isha and Karan were busy in talking. Frankly, I had never seen their mouth shut for even a single second. No one can ever guess what could be the topic of discussion for such a long time!

'You are getting weird dreams haan?' she said and smiled.

'Yes' I said, 'what do they keep talking about' I pointed at Isha and Karan.

'God knows. They never stop' she said. It was my time to execute my plan. I took out my hand and slowly moved it towards her's.

'Hey guys, what's happening' Ayesha popped out of nowhere destroying my perfectly romantic moment. I chained her with a thousand kilo RDX and blew her to pieces in my head for the ultimate sin she had done. I placed my hands back in the pocket.

'Nothing. Just talking' Mahira said as both of them smiled. I glared at her.

'What happened?' she asked. I shook my head.

DAMN!!! DAMN!! FUCKING DAMN!

'Bye guys. I am getting late. See you tomorrow! Bye Mahira' I said and smiled at her.

'Bye Sharief!' she gleamed and started walking away with Isha, Karan and the girl who just screwed my perfect plan, Ayesha.

I frowned and fished out my phone.

Sharief_Malhotra: **Do text me when you reach home okay?**

I pressed the send button. Unfortunately enough, 'Operation Hold Hands' wasn't executed that evening...

XV

Utsav Sharma

I crumpled the tissue paper and threw it in the commode.

It was tiring!

I press the flush thrice to ensure there are no remains of my crime left. I get out of the bathroom with my laptop still in my hands. Well, I know you might be wondering why the laptop when you have a phone?

The simple answer is, "Badi screen ka apna mazaa hai" (Large screen got its own pros).

I place the laptop on my bed and wash my hands with dettol. They say that only 0.1 per cent bacteria remains after one wash but 0.1 per cent bacteria in this case can result in increase of the total population by a unit. Lets not talk about it right now.

Sorry, I forgot to introduce myself. I am Utsav Sharma or Chocolate. The former one given by my parents and the latter one by my girlfriend. I am the son of two doctors but don't have the brain of even one! I am Sharief's best friend since ninth maybe. We were in the same tuition in ninth and in eleventh he opted Biology as one of his majors, making him my classmate again.

Two things I am going to get straight before beginning. First, I love Shah Rukh Khan though I am not a gay but will never refuse if offered to sleep with him and second, I love the internet for it was the place where I first texted the love of my life and the place where I searched 'Hot pics' for the first time before turning into a frequent shaker.

'Utsav' my mom called from downstairs. I put a straight face on and close the four tabs on my laptop that displayed the froth called 'porn' from various websites.

I bang close the door and rappel downstairs in full speed, rubbing my hands.

'Yes maa' I said as she was on her phone.

'Sharief. Talk to him' She said and handed me the phone. I went to the other corner of the room.

That cheap asshole. After rejecting my thirty five calls, ignoring my twelve texts, two days or for the way I measure time, nineteen Johnny Sin's videos later he calls me. 'I won't call you ever. Your girlfriend destroyed my perfect moment. You suck!' he had said to me.

'Finally the lovers reunite' I said as there was no reply from the other side.

'Look. I am sorry' he spoke in his usually calm voice.

'What? Got bored of your own hand? Need mine now? You better be sorry' I snapped as he cut me in mid sentence.

'Can I come to your home?' he said. I put the phone on hold and went near my mother.

'Maa can Sharief come home today?'

She rolled her eyes at me. It wasn't because of Sharief but it was because of me.

I had made a horrible image of 'Sharief Malhotra' in my home. My fake stories about him, his academic response and lacking of neuro motor skills were enough for my family to be convinced that *he took drugs and smoked pot.* From that day, everything that was wrong with me was blamed on him.

It started when the result of tenth class came. He got 8.8 CGPA but still managed to get a high end Smartphone from his parents whereas I got a perfect fucking 10 but didn't even get a *Mc Aloo Tikki* for it. I was angry and in pain too. I saw everyone around discussing smart phones in the class until one day when my patience lost its virginity and I snapped at my family with words that I termed were 'his'.

'I got a twenty five thousand worth new phone and what did you got huh? You didn't even got a new underwear or pair of socks for it! What is the fun of studying so much hard when the less smarter than you end up bagging goodies you never could' I had said to my family and didn't talked to them for two days.

After a real struggle of two days (for I didn't even saw a single porn), my family bought me a low end cheap Smartphone and termed Sharief as a typical *Iss sey dur reh tera career barbaad karega* kid! (Stay away from him, he'll end up screwing your career).

'Yes. You can come' I said, my mother still in her *woh haraami sach main aayega?* mode.

'Okay bye' he said and hung up.

'Anything else maa?' I said. She shook her head.

'Tell your useless friends to call you on your personal cell and not disturb us by paying useless visits to our house. I am going to the supermarket. Call me once he leaves' she said as I climbed the stairs and closed the door.

Okay, I am a hypocrite. I am not only guilty for whatever damage I have done to him in my family's eyes but also for being a double standard person. My family thinks that I am not on any social networking site whereas the truth is that I am a frequent user of Instagram. My family thinks that I study all day, locking myself in my room whereas the truth is that what I am doing is using the unlimited wifi and throwing tissue papers in the commode. My family thinks their child has never heard of something called 'girls' but I have a girlfriend and believe me, she's damn beautiful.

I had got her in my life because of him. Yes, because of Sharief. I know my words are enough to convince you that he is involved in flesh trade business but that cheap cute lovely asshole is involved in 'heart trade' business instead! I really love him from my heart but I don't think I can ever undo the damage I had done.

I locked the door and opened 'Google chrome' in my laptop with a fresh tissue paper in the other hand.

* * * *

Forty minutes and seven tissues later I heard a knock at the door. I opened it and saw Mr Malhotra standing there wearing a grey sweatshirt with 'batman' logo on it and blue jeans. He smelled great and if I were a gay, I would have kissed him.

'Look at yourself motherfucker!' He said and stepped into my room. He held his nose the moment he entered. His expressions were as same as the present condition of my room, 'disgusting'.

'What the hell are you doing? Close that' he spoke, his hand still on his mouth pointing to my laptop which still played a threesome video on it.

'Everyone does that' I said and stared my laptop like it was a portrait by some famous painter or something.

He went near my laptop and slapped its screen down.

'At least watch it on mute. Disgusting bastard' he said.

'Mute? Why do they add sound than?' I said.

He picked up a deodorant can from above the bed and sprayed it all over my room. He threw it back on the bed and removed his hand from mouth.

'Fuck you' he said as I picked all the tissue papers from around the room that could account for worth more than the total population of the country and threw them in the dustbin.

'Don't you bathe?' he said as he sat on the chair next to the bed.

'Twice' I said.

'Go lie to your mother! I know you well. Twice?' He said relaxing back in the chair.

'You didn't let me complete. I meant twice a year' I said and he giggled.

'I hope there is no traces of your kids on this chair' he said.

'I think you just sat on one of them.'

He stood up in a jerk and inspected the chair. He shook his head and stood up against the wall.

'Is there some place where you haven't done your Johnny Sins?' he said leaning against the wall.

'Here. On the bed. Because I do Mia Khalifa on bed' I said pointing to the bed on which I sat and was greeted with a middle finger.

'Stop your shit. I have some serious thing to talk about' he said with his expressions serious.

'I know. Ayesha screwed your perfectly romantic moment when you were going to hold Mahira's hand. How many more times do I need to hear this again and again' I said. I was literally bored for his old shitty story being repeated again and again.

'You don't understand. IT WAS THE PERFECT MOMENT!' He shouted.

'Easy tiger easy. Grab a tissue if you have some stress.'

'Shut up. Whatever she did was wrong' he said, eyes burning.

'Okay I admit. I am sorry from her side. Is that okay?' I said trying to resolve the situation a little.

'She will have to apologise. This is so unfair man!' He snapped.

'Okay, wait a second' I said and picked up my phone.

'Call Strawberry' I said to cortona as he made a face with expressions that honestly could be translated to *strawberry, my ass!*

'Ohhh Chocolate baby! Muahhh' The voice from the other side grunted unaware that the phone was on loud speaker. His eyes became big as if they were just going to pop out.

'Strawberry, I need a favour from you baby' I said.

'Ask for my life and I will give it to you' she said and a wide grin appeared on my face. Yes, I loved her madly and she loved me too. We were perfect for each other.

'Sharief's here. He wants to talk to you' I said, 'please apologize to him.'

'But I haven't did anything wrong!' she protested.

'Shh! Just do whatever I tell you to' I said and handed the phone to Sharief. He took three deep breaths which probably melted the rage inside him before speaking.

'Sharief' he spoke in his *I-control-everyone* tone.

'Sharief, I am sorry' she spoke just how he wanted to hear.

'You destroyed my perfect moment girl! You always do this to me and still you say "we are good friends". You still meet Diveesh, that son of a bitch even after I told you not to. You told Mahira I was going to propose her. There are way so many people in my life. Why is it only you the one who screws my happiness every time? Why? Do you have any personal grudge with me? You told me to stay away from Mohini. It must be you who had spoke some more shit about me just like he did! Do you hate me? Do you want us to not to be friends anymore. Okay, I accept that I am defeated. You never call me again and I'll never call you! Simple as hell!' he said with random emotions ranging through his face making it twitch like the ass I saw in the last video.

'Sharief? Are you there?' her voice sobbed. He ignored her. I was about to speak when the voice again started to speak.

'Thank you for bringing up this topic up today. So let me start from reminding you why we really are 'friends' or as you call us. There was a guy who helped me by giving his French textbook to me in class sixth and took the punishment on himself and stood for the whole period. There was a guy who helped me every time I needed despite me being rude and arrogant towards him. There was a guy who once gave me his almanac and got a parents note signed on it from the teacher and later tore it off' she said with little sobs in between. His face was expressionless and he was in deep thought. More deep than Rocco Reed had ever gone.

'I developed a mini crush on that guy. He was jolly, he made everyone happy and I cared for him. Not because he was my friend but because he was kind of my life. I told that guy not to engage in a relation with Mohini because I knew what kind of girl she was. Yes, I am a fucking imperfect person but that doesn't means that I don't care for you. I care for you and always will because…I love you…as a friend' she cried and laughed at the same time. A tear rolled down his eyes and a smile appeared on his face.

Wow! Even Sharief Malhotra cries!

'I am sorry' he finally spoke as the words choked him.

'You don't need to be sorry. I was wrong. I am sorry and I promise, I'll never disturb you in your personal life. I will never, ever in my life do that again' she said as I could sense her smile on the other side.

'I also promise one thing'

'What?'

'I'll never take your suggestions as orders' he said and laughed. He removed his glasses and kept it aside. It was kind of fun to watch 'Batman' cry.

'Mom's here. Got to go. Bye' she said as she hung up.

I saw Sharief. He was still there, leaning on the wall looking at the sky and smiling. It maybe the old memories that had hit him now.

He came to the bed and sat next to me.

'She's my girlfriend or yours? How can she say "I love you" to someone else?' I said and fake cried. He was a Drama queen but I was Sunny Leone in comparison to him.

'As a friend was also implied at the end' he spoke and laughed.

'Why are you here? Sitting next to me. I am in my shorts and you are in your jeans. I had seen this in some video, maybe xnxx.com. Two guys one bed, damn amazing!' I said bringing my knees close to my chest and holding on to them.

'You are such a pathetic son of a bitch' He said, 'Gay porn? Like seriously?'

'I never told you but I have interest in males. I have a crush on you from the day we first met. Can we do it, on the bed?' I said as he put his hands on my shoulders.

'Why not?' He said and laughed. A laugh not heard from a long time. A laugh that was powerful enough for the neighbours to mistake it as an orgasm. A laugh I loved.

'I love you man' He said hugging me.

'I love you too…as a friend' I said and returned him with a tighter hug.

'Hey, lets go to the Mall' he said and stood up from the bed collecting his glasses.

'Mall? I don't have the money' I said when in reality I had but I was saving it for Valentine's day.

'I have' he said as he stepped outside the room, 'wear some good clothes, wash your hands properly and apply some deodorant too' he shouted from the stairs.

* * * *

'Wave mall, bhaiya' He said to the driver who kept looking in the rear view mirror glancing regularly at me. I buttoned the top button of my shirt too as 'Fake taxi' videos just hit me hard.

'Why is he looking at me?' I whispered in his ears.

'Maybe wondering how can I have such a fucked up friend' I said as the driver sped off.

In thirty minutes we were there. The car stopped right near the entrance. We took the elevators to the third floor and got ourselves the tickets of 'Fifty shades of Black' the parody movie of 'Fifty shades of grey'.

'I heard this movie is lot more steamy than the real one' I said to him as the guard at security check pointed to my jean's pocket.

'What's in it?' he asked.

'This' I took out the three tissue papers I had taken along in case of emergency. The guard shook his head in horror.

'He has cold' Sharief said as we entered the cinemas. It was quiet and scarcely filled. Only a few young teenagers in search of new material to shake it were there. Well, what they never will realise that its India and the censors are sure to fuck the movie.

'Just ignore if something just splashes in air from nowhere' I said to him as we sat on our seats.

'Fuck you' he said and grabbed the popcorn, 'I am not going to give these to you for I don't trust you with your hands are clean or not.'

'They are absolutely clean' I said.

The movie was BORING. Yes, it sucked more than Sunny Leone. All the scenes were either cut or edited and the thing left can be honestly termed as 'Sex education for Kindergarten level'. We went to the Cafe Coffee day and ordered two Devil's own.

'Utsav, I have to ask you something' He said as we sat on the sofa.

'Yes'

'Am I a good person?' he spoke, lost in a world of his own. A question he has asked me maybe a zillion times.

'Yes you are' I said sipping from my coffee.

'Why do I feel like she is going to leave me?' He said with his expressions pale.

Look, this is the real problem with him. On one side, he is all cheered up and playful. A guy who doesn't cares for himself. A guy who wants to see everyone happy but on the other side, he is a depressed idiot who keeps on underestimating himself. He feels like he is the worst guy in the world. He is really the most confusing guy in the world.

'She won't. Simply won't. You are such a nice guy. She will never leave you. Just stay positive and be yourself. Even I have heard some people saying shit about you but trust me, I don't think it ever matters what people say. Love has nothing to do with people. It has only to do with a 'person'. Don't over think things dude. Here, want to watch some?' I said waving my phone at his face. He shook his head.

I pulled his cheek tightly, as tight as possible. He hated it when someone pulled his cheek. He turned red. More red than a spanked ass.

'Did you notice something?' I said. He smiled.

'What?'

'I pulled your cheek from my right hand' I said waving my right hand in air.

'Fuck you' he said in a harsh tone and sipped from his coffee.

XVI

I sat in my car and waved the living pervert a good bye. He grinned like an idiot. Sometimes I curse myself for making him date Ayesha. Part of me thanked god too, for he now had limited his single handed cardio exercises.

My phone buzzed. It was a call from the most beautiful girl in the world (I may spark a heavy controversy worldwide by saying this but for me, she is). I picked it up.

'Hey!' her voice greeted me. I smiled the moment I heard her voice.

This is literally one of the most idiotic things about love. Some voices, touches or even a glance can send chills down your spine and in my case, goose bumps too.

'Hey love!' I said, completely flattered by now.

'What are you doing?' she asked.

'Um...Nothing. Just dropped Utsav home after watching Fifty Shades of Black' I said.

'It's boring as fuck' she said after a little pause.

'Yes. You tell' I said.

'Can we go on a date tomorrow?' she asked in the loveliest tone possible.

Why would I say no? Why would I prefer to sit in a class with a blackboard filled with numerous unknowns and find their value instead of going on a date with the love of my life?

'Yes. We can. Absolutely' I said.

'WONDERFUL. We'll have to skip the school tomorrow' she said.

'There's no problem to it' I said, 'where do we go?'

'I'll tell you that tomorrow' she said. She was insane, surprising and lovable; all at once. I couldn't believe that I was dating her. That she was mine, forever.

'Okay. Had dinner?' I asked.

'Not yet. You know I told a friend of mine about us and he seemed so happy' she said.

He?

Now here is where the girls sometimes don't get the point. Boys are never jealous of each other. It's not in their genes. Jealousy is something only girl's posses. Still, whenever a girl tells her boy about some other guy, a feeling similar to jealousy arises in boys. We don't want to hear about him. No matter how much cute, loving or friend zoned the other guy is, we still hate it every time some other guy becomes the topic of discussion. Boys hate it!

'Okay. Why didn't you have your dinner? Its nine thirty already. You should have slept by now' I said in a worried tone. I care for her, that's all.

'I just don't feel like having it' she said.

'When do you feel like having food, Mrs Malhotra?' I said and heard a breath from the other side.

'Say that again'

'What?' I said, confused as fuck.

'Mrs Malhotra' she said. I could literally feel her blushing on the other side.

'Mrs Malhotra. Why don't you eat properly?' I said, a little gentle now stressing on the first word.

'Aww…That's so cute. As you say master, I'll have my food and sleep. Good night' she said.

'Good night love' I muttered after looking at the expressions of my driver who kept on checking me in the mirror.

'Just a friend' I said to him as he smiled.

The car reached home in another thirty minutes. I knocked at the door and my mother opened it. I smiled at her as I handed a box full of pastries to her.

'Here. For everyone' I said and smiled. Maybe love is the other name of happiness hormone.

'We've been waiting for you' she said. She was in her home clothes but still looked beautiful.

'I am sorry' I said. She smiled.

'There's something really keeping you from getting angry' she said and winked.

'And there's something really that's keeping me from entering my own house' I said and both of us laughed.

I stepped in and she bolted the door behind.

'Where's dad?' I said as I sat on the sofa.

'Doing what he usually does when he's home' she said and disappeared in to the kitchen.

'He usually scolds the living shit out of me. Where is he?' I said, a little louder enough to reach the kitchen.

'Watching news you idiot' she said as she came back with a glass of water. I drank it all at once.

She sat on the sofa with some Hindi novel in her hand. She loved Hindi literature.

I stood and went to their room. I could hear voice of a crime anchor telling the viewers to be a little more aware of them. I opened the door a little.

'*Aao ji Aao*' he said the moment he saw me. Though there was no trace of anger on his face, I still had my balls in my mouth.

'What happened?' I asked him.

'Mr Scientist. Looks like you are living in the 4th dimension' he said.

'And what makes you say this?' I said in a balanced tone.

'You have forgotten the concept of time completely. There's no time for you. Look at the watch' he said. It was ten o'clock now.

'I am sorry dad' I said. These mother fucker crime shows should fucking end. They are the main reason why Indian parents don't trust their kids nowadays. Come home late by an hour, the whole family thinks you are a serial killer.

'Where have you been?' he said after a brief dramatic pause when I expected him to slap me.

'Out with Utsav' I said.

'Okay. May I ask you a question?' he said with his expressions serious. He still was in his office clothes that signified that he was the boss. At office and at home too.

'Yes please' I said.

'Do you have a girlfriend? Don't lie to me' he said looking straight into my eyes.

'I…I don't…I simply don't have a girlfriend. That's all' I said as I struggled to make a straight and innocent face.

'Then why are your grades so low?' he said. He never had mentioned grades in the past four years. What was making him do so?

'Dad, I am no Einstein. I get more marks than my friends. Isn't that enough?' I said in a reflex and then bit my tongue.

'That's not at all enough. From any standards. Why don't you concentrate just on your studies? Vanshika's both daughter scored high in board examinations. And what did Gourav do? Hit the gym, impressed beautiful girls and all? You are on his footsteps. I should warn you son' he said.

I nodded and looked down. I wanted to jump and hit my head on a glass pane at that moment.

'Go and sleep. School *jaana hai kal'* he said.

'I am not going to school tomorrow' I said. His eyes turned big.

'And why is it so?' he said.

'Just don't feel like going' I said. He shook his head. My heart clenched as I expected a tight slap to sting my cheeks any moment. Fortunately enough, it didn't happen.

'This is the last warning for you' he said as I nodded and left the room. I opened my room and bolted it from inside.

After half an hour thinking about what I will wear tomorrow, I fell asleep.

* * * *

The alarm clock rang to life. I was still half asleep. I took it in my hand and threw it. The sound of the breaking glass broke my sleep immediately. I jumped off my bed and passed a disappointed look after seeing the condition of the alarm clock. My vision shifted to the wall clock at the other corner of the room. It was ten of the morning.

I unplugged my phone which now had more charge percentage than I ever had got in any exam of my life and called Mahira.

After four rings, she picked it up.

'Hey love!' she said her voice sweeter and seductive than ever. Girls are seductive when half asleep, no offence.

'Good morning!' I said.

'Just woke up' she said.

'When do we go?' I asked. There was a brief pause at the other side.

'Give me an hour' she said.

An hour? Like seriously? I could get dressed in five minutes even including brushing and having a shower. Females, I tell you, live in the fourth dimension. A dimension where time has no value. Just like the purse they purchased last week.

'And where exactly are we going?' I asked searching for my purse.

'Going somewhere where we don't need money to buy happiness' she said as a little electric shock hit me. Girls make the best guess at the right time.

'Okay. See you soon' I said and hung up. I brushed and then went to the washroom for a shower. I trimmed my beard after wards and smiled while looking at the mirror.

I dressed into a red T-shirt and my same old blue jeans. Red, for she loved red and I loved her. I straightened my hairs in the mirror until I looked like 'Gareebon ka Arjun Kapoor'. I cleaned my spectacles and wore them to make my face even worse.

'Where are you going?' my mother said as she saw me checking myself in the mirror.

'Some work' I said and smiled.

'I hope you don't return at ten again today' she said and passed a fake smile, 'moreover the driver has gone for a leave.'

'No problem. I'll hail an auto' I said as words ate me up.

Auto? On my first date? Who goes on a date on an auto?

What if she feels little and pity for me?

What if she cancels our date?

Why the fuck did the driver had to leave only today?

I fake smiled at her. She fake smiled at me. No matter fake, they still were smiles at least.

'I'll be back soon' I said and hugged her. She smiled, a real one this time and I came out of my home.

It was the early days of February and the sun was still high on dope. Still, I could see many people wearing winter clothes mainly sweaters and sweat shirts. Poor they.

It took me five minutes to find an autowala that agreed to go to her place in feasible amount of money.

'Gandhi Nagar bhaiya' I said as he nodded and started to drive through the tight lanes of my area.

Twenty minutes and ninety curses later, I was there. I told the autowala to stop just a little before her house to avoid suspicion. I fished out my phone and called her.

She picked up in the first ring.

'Coming' she said. I smiled and in five seconds, she was there. Outside of her house wearing blue shades and a red T-shirt with denim jeans. She looked for me but couldn't find me

'Hey!' I said as I came near her. She hugged me tightly. I knew the difference between our frames so I decided not to hug her back tightly, else it would have resulted in some serious bone injury of hers.

'Missed me?' I asked.

'Always' she said and smiled.

'Where's the car?' she said.

I mentally beheaded myself for not bringing a car.

'Sorry…But the car wasn't available…So I took an…' I said as she cut me mid way.

'AUTO! Wohoo! That's really bad ass and little like the date of my dreams!' she said pointing to the auto with child like excitement. I found no sarcasm in her voice. Maybe I was wrong.

We sat in the auto. The driver threw a confused look at us.

'*Kidhar jaana hai bhaiya?*' he said looking at me, who was still busy in examining the mysteriously beautiful creature sitting right next to me.

'*Sir ji!*' He said as she shook me and laughed.

'*Madame se pucho bhaiya*' I said giving an all knowing smile.

'Church *chalo*' she said as a laugh literally escaped out of my mouth.

'What?' she said irritated and in pain.

'Sorry but Madame, who goes to Church on their first date? You know that I don't believe in this nonsense right?' I told to her, still laughing.

'We go to Church. *Bhaiya aap chalao*' she said and punched me playfully.

'But Mahira…' I said.

She didn't reply. Just rested her head on my shoulder. It felt wonderful. And as the things could only get better, the auto started playing an old romantic song. I held her hand tightly as her fingers intervened into mine. Her hairs touched my lap and she looked cute, beautiful, irritating, anarchist and so many god damn fucking things at once. I wanted to kiss her right now but didn't wanted the autowala to crash in some car while seeing a scene like straight out of those Emraan Hashmi movies.

The sun didn't felt hot any longer. The autowala coughed occasionally whenever our faces came a little closer. I should have slapped him with a five hundered rupee note had I known that things will be going to turn so romantic.

I took out my phone and read out random quotes and shayaries I have written for her last night.

She found it cute and smiled. Maybe it was due to our first close encounter, I noticed dimples on her right cheek.

'You are beautiful' I murmured in her ear, her head still resting on my shoulder.

'I know that, right?' she said.

'I was joking' I said as her hand landed on my cheek.

'Shut up' she said and removed her head from my shoulder.

'It felt good' I said, frowning.

'You were not joking, right?' she said and laughed. Her perfect lips now almost distracting the living shit out of me.

'You are the most beautiful girl I have ever met' I said as she smiled. Our eyes matched each other and there was a stare game going on.

She closed her eyes, still smiling. I smiled and slowly started bringing my face closer to hers, my eyes still closed.

'*Lo bhaiya. Pahunch gaye hum*' the autowala said as both of us startled. If I had the contact of the ISIS chief, I would have straight away called him and sent that autowala to Syria to get his body splattered with bullets.

Both of us passed him an embarrassed smile. We got out of the auto and I paid. She used her bargaining superpowers which resulted in me paying fifty rupees less.

I never visited a church, unless it was Christmas. Visit only once a year and expect that god will fulfil all your wishes. I guess that's what most of us do, right?

It was mostly empty. There was no crowd at the gate. She put her shades in her purse and smiled at me.

'Seriously? What are we going to tell our kids? We went to 'Church' on our first date? So romantic' I said and laughed. She made a face.

'It's not funny' she said as we walked through the gate.

I stopped mid way. She turned towards me and passed a confused look.

'What?' she said.

'I don't believe in God and shit. Why am I here then?' I asked her. I was an Atheist, I am and I will stay. God is a concept for pity and scared people. Those not strong enough to take all the stress and responsibility, throw them on God.

'Why can't you just follow me? Without speaking anything' she said. I smiled and took her hand in mine.

'Shadow always follows you but only when you are in the limelight. Guess what, I am better than your shadow' I said. The dimples appeared again on her cheek.

I followed her. We walked upstairs, to the chapel. It was quiet and peaceful. I saw the father sitting, reciting some holy verse and the sister smiled at us the moment we entered the chapel.

We sat in the last row. I ran my eyes through the walls of the chapel. They had some old scriptures and paintings of Jesus Christ with a little message written on the bottom.

My eyes shifted to her. She sat there, breathing as low as possible, her eyes closed and looking more adorable than ever. She murmured little things in between her slow breaths.

I placed my hand on my chin and kept looking at her. The father, at the other corner, looked up at me and smiled. I returned him with another smile, maybe a little less holy and religious.

She smiled the moment she noticed what I was doing. I was lost in her. Looking at her face is something I can do for lifetime. Though those lips did the little job of polluting my brain with the possibilities in the spiritual and religious environment, I could still keep looking at her face, her eyes which appeared a little more attractive when closed, her ears, and her cute nose. Everything.

'Stop it now!' she said in a low tone, still smiling.

'I can't help it' I said and smiled.

'This is god's home. See' she said, pointing to the father who still was reading verses.

'We are no different. He's in love with God. I am in love with you' I said and she blushed.

'Aw...You fiction writer!' she said and pulled my cheeks.

'My words are fiction but feelings are absolutely true' I said. *Don't know why but people never trust writers easily just because they manipulate with words? Oh come one!*

'Why don't you believe in god?' she asked, staring right in my eyes.

'It's my choice. I am atheist by choice' I said.

'Have you taken the moral responsibility of everyone around you? Have you ever felt helpless and then blame it all on you?' she asked, her face calm.

'Um...Yes. When my great grandmother died, I stood there. I could do nothing but look at her and curse myself. With every breath, I blamed myself even more. I had nothing to do with her. I was alone, I needed help. I wanted to call ambulance but was panicked. What else do you expect?' I said in a single breath.

'Yes. This is where you lack. You took all the blame on yourself. You could have remained calm, helped the situation but from your words...she must be really old. And it's the law of nature and god, people who are born have to die. Why are you so upset from your life?' she said and held my hand.

'Because it sucks. God sucks. Religion sucks. One moment we are here, hand in hand, talking bull shit about love. The other, any terrorist can blow the living shackle out of this place and kill us. For no reason. I see people on road, begging, getting kicked by rich tards. I see people in five star hotels, eating nothing because of being on dieting. Ours is one fucked up world. Those who want food sleep hungry and those who have the money to afford the food and other fancy things to take up their ass, are on dieting. It's because of your God. Had he planned the world carefully and fairly, it would have been one happy place we would have been living in' I said, a little loud.

'Who are you? Batman? Superman? You can do nothing by yourself. You can take small initiatives, act better and increase your own standard of living. Though this is called as being 'selfish' but we do need to act a little selfish sometimes. If you spend your time thinking about other people, when will you live your own life? It's gone in a moment. Like Whoosh. You do nothing but regret in the end for mistakes you never committed. That's why we have God here. I don't know if he exists or not, but he surely gives me a sense of motivation and I can throw some of my problems on him, making my own life better and stress free' she said.

Maybe she was right. Why should I think about the world? Does the world even know a guy named Sharief Malhotra who is madly in love with a girl exists? Probably not. All I could do is take a small step.

'May I ask a question again?' I said. She raised her eyebrow.

'Why are we sitting in a Church on our first date?' I asked. She threw her hand in air.

'Whenever I am stressed or my mood is off, I go to the chapel and sit there. Even in our school. It's a really energetic yet peaceful environment in here. See, we are happy without sipping over priced coffees, fake accents and air-conditioned rooms. We are happy without money. This is the best place I could think about. We could also had hit some park but you know...there are people and people and people, and they stare you like only you are the one with two eyes, two ears and one nose' she said in an extremely cute way. I laughed. I wanted to lean forward and kiss her, now that things were out of control but thought that I could get a straight wild card entry to hell for my action and didn't wanted to regret it later.

'I love you Mahira' I said, looking straight into her eyes.

'I love you too' she said, 'Auto's are a little less private. Let's take a taxi home' and winked.

I didn't get the pun though I still was a little turned on.

XVII

We sat in the taxi. I checked my watch. It was four of the evening.

'We can go to coffee shop if you want to' I said. She shook her head.

'I told you enough times that I don't need such fancy things' she said and smiled.

'Bhaiya can you please keep driving straight and drop us on the bridge?'I said as the car driver brought the car to a halt.

'But you said we are going home....' Mahira said as the driver passed a confused look.

'It's my turn now' I said and she smiled. I nodded to the driver's expressions and he started to drive.

I held her hand more tightly. She smiled. The feel of her skin against mine was incomparable. The warmth her skin provided could even put sun to shame.

It took five more minutes to reach the bridge. The driver stopped the car at a side.

Like a complete gentlemen, I ran to her side and opened the door for her. She stepped out like a queen. She was the queen of my life. The queen of my world.

I paid the driver as he shook his head for wasting his time. I paid him, right? Who is he then to think that I wasted his time?

We passed each other glittering smiles, our fingers still intervened stronger than super glue. I pointed an empty corner of the bridge to her. We walked slowly looking at the people.

The bridge was almost full of cars. Thanks to engineering, it was able to take the stress the cars exerted on it. There were a variety of people on the bridge. Some couples, some with their families, some alone sunk in a deep thought. The cool breeze blew as the sound of the Tawi's water added a layer of romance to the environment.

Her hair flew. Though they weren't long enough to touch my face, I stepped a little closer to her, just inches away. I looked into her eyes. The face that I could keep staring till infinity was now lit up with a smile. I brought my face a little closer.

'People are staring us' she said and smiled.

'So what, we are stars. People generally keep staring them for hours, right?' I said and she blushed.

'Yes…I love you' she said.

'What makes you say that again and again?' I asked her, laughing.

'Maybe I won't be there the next moment. That's why' she said looking down.

I hugged her tightly. As tight as possible and released her a few seconds later fearing that she'll choke.

'Nobody dares to take you away from me. Nobody' I said, anger bursting in my eyes as I imagined the situation.

She leaves me alone in this world. Alone.

'Sharief…' she said. I didn't maintain eye contact, still angry.

'Sharief…Look at me' she said again.

'No. I won't. You keep talking that you'll leave me. You know how much I love you, right?' I said.

'Yes. I know how much you love me. But trust me, I love you a little more' she said and I laughed.

'Please. *Date pe bhi church jaane waali ladki!*' I said and she laughed. She rubbed her hands as the atmosphere started to cool. It was my best shot at trying what they generally do in Movies. I removed my jacket and placed it on her. She blushed.

'Watching quite some romantic movies, eh?' she said 'And that church thing, oh please. It would have been better if you had a girlfriend that made you run like dog behind her, holding shopping bags and making you spend your lungs out. Want me to be like that? Eh? Eh?'

'Never would I want you to change. You are my Mahira. I just love the way you are' I said. She smiled wide and her eyes glittered.

'Perfect match hai boss' I heard someone say. Both of our eyes shifted to a cute little guy, fair complexion, dressed in a school uniform, his shirt out of his pant staring at us with a toothpick in his mouth. His clothes were full with dust.

'Hey. Thank you! You are so cute!' Mahira said and bended down to pull the cheeks of that guy.

'Sorry but I already have a girlfriend' he said and both of us laughed. He passed a flying kiss to both of us and left as we waved at him. The level of sarcasm he threw on us didn't match his age. He walked slowly, his eyes closed acting like a mature guy who just fought with his wife. We laughed again.

'He's sooo cute' she said. I frowned.

'I thought I was the only "sooo cute" in this world' I said and faked expressions of being hurt.

'Aw…Inferiority complex' she said and winked.

'Huh!' I said.

'You are soooo cute' she said and pulled my cheeks.

Had it been Utsav or any other random girl, I would've thrown her off the bridge for pulling my cheeks. It hurts. Only the people with chubby cheeks will get my pain. It was Mahira and I was hers.

'What if I…' I said and shook my head.

'What?' she said puzzled.

'Kiss you. Here, in the middle of the traffic' I said looking straight into her eyes. I couldn't believe it was the same Sharief Malhotra which feared from even holding hands. Love gifts us all with a little frankness.

'You want these cars to ram into each other? I bet no one could bear such a romantic site' she said.

'Yes. And let me tell you, those lips are really distracting' I said.

'I know right' she said and laughed.

She was no different from the other girls. She laughed the same way they did. She behaved almost the same way. She had the same genotype and phenotype they possessed. I don't know why but listening to her laughter, staring her face for hours made me feel butterflies in my stomach, holding her hand tightly so that she could never escape. This is love ladies and gentlemen.

'What do you want to do in future?' I asked her.

'What do you want me to say? The typical answer or the honest one' she asked. I scratched my head in confusion.

'I didn't get you' I said.

'The typical answer is the one I usually tell my relatives and family. Study hard, get into a medical college, become a doctor, practise for a while, marry, have kids and die' she said.

'And what about the honest answer?' I said.

'Honest one is straight from the heart. Only some of my friends have heard it' she said.

'Would you mind if there's an addition of your boyfriend in the list too?' I said and she smiled.

'No...Okay. I want to become a doctor, earn a little and then travel the world' she said.

'Travel the world?' I asked.

'Yes. Away from all this middle class bull shit, away from my life, explore new places, meet new people, live my life' she said.

'And who are you going to take along with yourself?' I asked.

'You' she said and smiled. My face lit up with a smile, flashing my teeth.

'What if I am not there?' I said. She shook her head and gripped my hand a little tighter.

'You will be' she said, 'tell me what you've planned about the future?'

'I...I really don't know what I will do with my future' I said.

'You must have taken this stream with something in your mind' she said.

'Yes. Actually I love biology but more importantly, Mohini had opted for the same' I said.

Had it been a boy, he would have acted like a total asshole upon the mention of old love. Thank god she was a girl. She smiled.

'I am thinking of becoming a writer' I said.

'You write really sexy...Oh sorry, I know you hate that word. You write damn amazing!' she said

'How do you know I hate that word?' I said.

'Whenever someone says sexy, you throw a fake smile' she said.

I smiled, a real one full of joy.

'I don't want my kids to look at their friends and feel sorry for their father who earns almost nothing from writing' I said, 'my wife to complain that my royalties are not enough for her fancy shopping'

'You know your wife doesn't like fancy things don't you. Though I love shopping' she said. I blushed.

'Only if my wife gives me the permission' I said.

'Your wife has already given you the permission, honey' she said and I smiled.

'What will you write? Like writing Shayaries and Short stories and writing books are two different things' she said. I nodded.

'Don't know. Maybe I'll write about you' I said.

'You already have written so much about me. My friends just blush to death when I make them read your stories' she said.

'What am I going to write about? There was a book I started but never wrote more than 3,000 words. It was a shitty concept though. On friendship and hatred' I said.

'Try writing a love story' she said.

'Like ours?'

'Yes. Why not write our love story. It would be funny and romantic at the same time' she said, 'add a little tragic angle too. Like yours and Mohini's. People love heartbreak stories. They are the bestsellers right?'

'I will write something. Now please end this topic. I'll think about the writing field. I suck at writing, don't know why some people find my works amazing.'

'You are the best writer in the world!' she said and curled herself around my arm.

'What about being the best boyfriend?' I asked as we walked slowly on the bridge.

'Um...No, I don't think so. My friend's have already got better boyfriends' she said and laughed out loud.

The fact that there are seven billion people on earth but you fall for only one because of their smile, laughter, lips always disturbs me!

We talked endlessly about things that mattered the least as the sun started to set in front of us, our fingers intervened and so do our souls. Aliens, love, sex, universe, movies, porn, incognito mode and so on; I wanted the time to freeze. I wanted to keep looking at her, her smile, keep hearing her sweet voice, looking at her distracting lips while I figure out numerous ways of kissing her. Every male is pervert.

I checked my watch. It was 7:00 of the evening.

'I think I should drop you home now' I said.

'No! I don't want to go. I want to be with you' she said.

'See the time. Your family must be waiting for you' I said.

'Yes. I'll pay for the auto this time' she said and I laughed.

'Girls don't pay on dates. Boys generally do' I said and took out my wallet.

'I am not "Girl". The typical one. I am Mahira Bhatt, understand?' she said raising her eyebrow and slapping my hand playfully.

'Okay Miss. As you wish' I said and hailed an auto.

Though the auto drove way too much slowly, it felt like I was in the fourth dimension where time flew faster. I didn't want the day to end. In some ten minutes, we reached her home.

She kept sitting next to me even after the auto had stopped. It was clear that even she didn't want to leave.

'Come on baby, cheer up' I said.

'I don't want to leave' she said in a child like tone, her arms crossed.

'Don't behave like a child Mahira' I said.

'I love you naa. I don't want to go' she said.

'I love you too naa' I said. She avoided eye contact.

I got out of the auto and waited for her. Three minutes of melodrama later, she got out of it. Girls always know something even if they think know nothing. It's Melodrama.

'Bye…I am sorry' she said loudly as the auto started.

'Sorry for what?'

'Come on. I am a girl. I am allowed a little melodrama sometimes' she said and I laughed.

'It was the best day of my life' we both said in unison. She smiled.

'Bye!' I said as she passed a flying kiss. Both of us smiled and the auto drove off. I missed her already.

It took me another twenty minutes to reach home. The roads were now a little less noisy but even more cars were visible now. Though the cars still honked, it had no effect on me. I was already lost in recalling today. I missed our closeness, her face, her words, her touch but more importantly I missed her. It was really the best date of my life. It was my first date. I was damn excited to tell all of my friends that we went on a date to a church.

'Thank you' I said to the autowala as I got out of the auto. He smiled.

'I too had a girlfriend…when I was your age' he said.

'What now?' I asked him.

'I don't have her as my girlfriend now' he said. He was hardly twenty five.

'Oh…I am so sorry' I said trying my best to put on a sad face.

'I have her as my wife now' he said and I smiled.

He took out his wallet from the pocket of his pant and showed me a photograph. It was a collage of two photos. One was of theirs when they used to be young, of my age. The other was of their marriage. I smiled at him and handed him the photograph back.

'Sometimes love finds a way itself' he said and winked. He ignited the engine and drove off, leaving smoke on my face with a brilliantly lit smile too.

I pressed the door bell thrice and later realised that we were so busy with our lives, that we didn't even had enough time to get the bell repaired or replaced. Yes, we had time to discuss diamond rings, Vanshika aunty's daughter's marks, quality of food in Ankit's marriage but not enough to get the door bell repaired.

I knocked hard.

'Dad! Mom!' I shouted as I knocked at the door. There was no response.

I knocked again as at that very moment, mom opened the door.

'He's angry again with you' Mom said.

'Who's angry with me?' I asked her.

'Your father' she said.

I stepped inside the house on my toes, making least noise as possible. One could easily hear the "Mission Impossible" theme song being played in the background. I controlled my laughter and walked slowly to my room.

'Mr Malhotra' I heard from behind as I stopped at that very instant. My body froze, heart stopped beating.

I turned back and saw my father standing there, smiling at me.

Why is he smiling? He should be angry, standing with some stick to beat the living shackle out of me. The fact that he was smiling didn't go down with me.

'Where have you been, Mr Malhotra. Long time no see' he said and laughed. He was in his home clothes.

My mind searched 'Excuses' on Google. Unfortunately it was offline. Nerve impulses rushed in my brain thinking for the least silly excuse possible.

'um…I was with Gourav' I said.

'Oh…That's good then. Gourav!' he called his name as the Greek god emerged out of my room dressed in a dark blue T-shirt and blue jeans.

'How come he was with you? You are here since three' my father said almost suppressing a smile.

'Hi Gourav' I said with fake enthusiasm. He passed a *confused as fuck* look.

'Not this Gourav dad. Gourav Chabra. My friend' I said as he let out a laugh.

'Never heard about him from you before' he said, raising an eyebrow. I signalled Gourav to operate the escape plan as soon as possible. It was up to him. He will pull me out of this shit. He always comes up with some idea and then saves me from the ultimate wrath.

He nodded and walked upstairs, telling my dad that he wants to pee.

'Yes. As I was saying, I have never heard about this Gourav Chabra from you before. Where does he live?' he asked, still smiling.

I wanted to ask him why he was smiling. Maybe he knew everything and now was pretending that he didn't and wanted to enjoy the situation a little.

'I…He…lives in Gandhi…' I said as my phone rang. It was from Gourav.

I deliberately put it on loud speaker.

'Hey Sharief!' he said in a changed voice. Even I wasn't able to recognise his voice. Fucker must have been doing some research on Batman stuff.

'Hey Gourav' I said in a fake tone.

'The day it was…amazing! I hope you have reached home now' he said, fake coughing.

'Yes. It was. Let's meet some other day too. It's always nice meeting you' I said.

'Yes buddy. Take care of yourself. Bye' he said and disconnected the call.

'Now I see' my dad said and smiled wide. He shook his head and smiled again.

What the hell was wrong with him?

'We are going for a dinner outside in an hour from now. Your clothes look extra fine. Wait for us to get dressed' my dad said and patted my shoulder. He disappeared inside his room.

Gourav came downstairs exactly seven minutes later.

'You are my saviour' I said and hugged him tightly kissing his cheek.

'Okay okay okay…please' He said and hugged me even tighter.

'Where were you exactly?' he asked.

'We are going for a dinner, right? I will tell you whatever happened today there. We generally have nothing to do other than to listen Anti Pakistani talks of our parents' I said and he laughed.

'I never help anyone for free' he said. I took out my wallet from the back pocket of my jeans.

'Hey' he protested, 'I don't need money. Just do me a favour' he said.

'What favour?' I asked.

'The one that you usually do' he said and I frowned. It must be a girl again.

'But I have a girlfriend now…I don't want to feel it anymore. I already have someone who loves me' I said. Being born in gym and looks of Greek god, the girls went gaga over him. They found out his whatsapp number and then texted him. He made me sometimes to text the girl because he was too busy with his girlfriend. Funny how girls still flirted even after he told them that he already had a girlfriend and that they were serious for each other.

When I didn't had a girlfriend, I used to chat with those girls acting like I was Gourav and felt the love and flirt they had for him. It felt wonderful. Being loved though virtually. Now it was a different thing though. I didn't needed to be Gourav Malhotra for someone to text me "I love you". There was already someone who loved me. The real me.

'Here' he gave me his phone with Whatsapp already opened. For the next half an hour, until my family got well dressed enough to visit a five star hotel, I chatted with the girl.

My phone rang, It was from Mahira.

'Reached home?' she said the moment I picked up the call.

'Yes' I said. She was caring.

'Going out to have dinner with my family. Take care, I love you' she said…

'I love you too' I said and disconnected the call.

No matter how much ugly, fucked up, idiotic, pervert I was, there was someone to love me. And that someone made me blush every time I thought about her!

XVIII

'Are they here?' my mother asked me. We were now all dressed for our once in a week five star restraint appearance. She was still in her room, trying jewellery that would compliment her beauty even more as Dad, my sister and Gourav sat in the living room waiting for Gourav's parents to come.

'Not yet' I said through the bolted door.

She unbolted the door. Dressed in a black suit with earrings that were carefully selected, she looked stunning.

'How do I look?' she asked me.

'Is there any way I couldn't say 'Perfect'?' I said as she pulled my cheeks.

'Where are they? They gave us the time of eight and see, they are late themselves' she said.

I went to the living room and saw Gourav texting some random girl, my dad checking his e-mail and my sister playing Candy Crush on my phone.

'Call your mom. Why are they not here yet?' I said to Gourav who carefully, not getting caught by my father waved his middle finger at me. He was a little angry with me for not telling him where exactly I was or what exactly I did the whole day.

At that moment, three consecutive car honks were heard as his parents arrived. I locked the gate as everyone sat in the new SUV his father had bought just yesterday. I had a special place in my heart filled with hatred for SUVs. Maybe it was because of Umaan.

'Namaste' I said as I touched the feet of his parents. They exchanged blessings. I and Gourav were made to sit in the back trunk of the car. It's seriously the worse place to sit because your head keeps on bumping and bumping while your legs struggle for space. When two people sit together, the situation is even worse and reminds of some scene from a B grade movie with legs intervened....Um...Leave it.

One of Gourav's sisters sat on my mother's lap and the other on her mother's.

The car drove fast as his father kept hitting the automatic weather sensing system button again and again in an attempt to show off his new car. My dad rolled his eyes. My head bounced and hit the roof thrice. I wanted to teleport to the restaurant skipping this fearful journey which was more dangerous than one of the tasks in "Fear factor".

Gourav was still on his phone. What he couldn't see was that his phone's screen was visible in the window behind. He was watching Game of Thrones. Though he concentrated less on the story and his hands were always on the forward button.

'By the time we reach there, I'll be deader than John Snow' I said as he startled.

'What?'

'Nothing...Carry on' I said. To make the situation worse, Gourav's dad started playing old Mohammad Rafi songs with lyrics that were more difficult to memorize than the whole modern periodic table.

In twenty five minutes we were there. As I stepped out of the car, I saw the fucked up expressions of the other people in the parking. Well, it really deserves that kind of expression when you see nine people, mostly adults, getting out of an SUV. Middle class people know how to manage.

'My legs are asleep' Gourav said and shook them vigorously, 'Fuck. I could have taken an auto instead.'

'Hey. Control your voice. This is a restaurant' I said as my father got out of the car.

'You are so slim and lean. Look at me. My head hurts. I thought I would even forget to recall your names' I said and rubbed my head.

'You are not that fat. Shut up.'

'Yes. I know what you were doing in there. Game of thrones huh?' I said and rolled my eyes.

'It has got a lot of action' he said and winked.

'Action?' I asked a little confused.

'You are a kid. Leave it' he said and squeezed my shoulder. I wanted to punch him but he was the Greek god and I don't think I could have matched his moves. Gourav went to his father and talked about the level of comfort we had in journey. His father nodded but frankly, from his expressions, he gave a flying fuck.

'See. How much they show off. Like they come to restaurants every day' my mother mumbled from behind as his father handed the car keys to valet and smiled.

'Please mom. Be a little...' I said as she cut me mid way.

'Yes. Now even my seventeen years son wants me to live my life his way. God' she said. I excused myself from any more melodrama and went on to join Gourav again.

'My phone's battery is at nine per cent' he said as he waved his phone at my face.

'Thanks heaven' I said and looked at the sky to add a dramatic effect.

We entered the hotel and did what every middle class family does first, after entering a five star hotel. I mean clicking pictures.

All of us except me and Gourav were now frenzy. They clicked photographs from their phone like there's going to be no tomorrow, that too in weird poses. I wished to god for not bumping into one of my school mates here, for my 'ALIEN' family would become the topic of discussion till the next year.

Exactly fifteen minutes, thousand photos and many megabytes later, we stepped in the elevator as my father pressed the button for the seventh floor.

We were in KC Residency. It is a five star hotel with a revolving restaurant at the top. It was the same hotel where Ankit's ring ceremony had taken place.

No silence can ever match the one Indian families have in elevators. Everyone is looking up then down and then when they can't think of anything else, they fish out their phone and keep doing random shit.

Thirty seconds later, the door opened as every one of us finally took a breath. Though I felt that Gourav's father kind of touched my behind deliberately but later dismissed the thought after looking at his three children.

'We have already booked a table in the name of Mr Malhotra' my mother said, in a superior tone to the manager who greeted us with folded hands. Indians love to show off their superiority sometimes. He nodded and accompanied us to a table.

In just a fraction of seconds, all of us were busy in our little world. My dad sat with Gourav's, my mother with her mother, my sister though she was little had the same interest in Siddarth Malhotra movies as her sisters sat with them and I sat with a guy whom I could do nothing but admire, even if I am not gay.

'How do you get these muscles?' I said as his biceps and triceps looked a little more developed than the last time. He was still on his phone. I wanted to snatch his phone and throw it out at escape velocity so it could never come back.

'What?' he said as he placed his phone on the table.

'How did you get these?' I said squeezing his arm. It was really nothing as compared to me.

'Um...Work out and a few protein shakes. That's all' he said and smirked, 'look at that girl man. So damn beautiful' almost pointing at the girl sitting just two more tables away.

'What?' I said and looked at the girl. I startled, jumping from my seat making the glass on the table fall. It was all water on the table. It was her. Miss Bhat.

'What the fuck' I said loud enough for Gourav's father to hear.

'What did you said beta?' he asked with suspicious expressions.

'Uh...I am sorry for that. I just want to say something' I said, my eyes still on that beautiful creature. She was dressed in a white T-shirt and black jeans. She looked beautiful. Maybe it was her beauty that made the sun burn with jealousy every day.

Her head turned towards me and a frozen expression appeared on her face. The ice was broken by her smile. She was sitting with her father and brother. She half waved at me as the rest two on her table were busy in talking something serious. I wanted to pass her a flying kiss but restrained myself. She smiled at me again and again.

Gourav looked at me and whispered 'What the fuck'.

'Yes please' he said as everyone on the table looked at me with puzzled expressions.

'Um...' I said as she gestured me with a '*What the hell are you doing?*'

'We are listening' he said and cleared his throat as I kept staring her. She pointed towards her ear maybe telling me she was listening.

'Okay. So let me get some things straight. I have been observing some really beautiful things around me' I said as she laughed.

'Like what?' the elder one among Gourav's sisters said. All the ears were now turned to me.

I kept staring at that beautiful face. It was really God's way of telling me that she really loved me. We were here, again, together though a few tables apart. I couldn't stop myself from blushing like an idiot after seeing her smile every time.

'Like…nature' I said as she held her mouth with her hand, almost controlling her laugh.

'What? We are really not getting you' my father said with his trademark raised eyebrow.

'Have all of us seen our surroundings? How much beautiful they are? No. What we are doing is finding happiness in that little five inch screen that runs on battery. Why are we doing this? How many of us love nature? Frankly nobody does. We do nothing but make the problem worse. Global warming, over population, deforestation…So many things we are guilty of. I guess that no matter how much five star this restaurant is, it was built after cutting a few trees and displacing few wild animals from their place. From their home. We should take up actions. Actions that could make our life better. The nature is so beautiful, lovable, cute, adorable, and kissable that we just can't ignore her. Yes, I love her and will love her till my last breath because she is mine!' I said as everyone burst into claps. She blushed and then clapped too, producing a little whistle from those perfect lips; her father and brother still lost in some serious discussion. I had not taken my eyes off her for even a single moment.

Though my words sounded from some hardcore environmentalist, I was talking about her. I am no more different. I don't really give a flying fuck about nature like everyone nowadays.

The others on the table appreciated my concern towards nature.

'It must be the side effect of studying Biology all the time' my mother said.

'It's a side effect of love' I wanted to say.

'You missed something' Gourav said as I sat back, still looking at her, our eyes locked.

'What?' I said looking at him.

'That nature is dressed in white T-shirt and black jeans' he said and laughed a hysterical laughter. I shook my head and sipped water directly from the bottle.

I punched his stomach. He laughed again.

I relaxed back in the chair and kept looking at her, lost in a world of my own imagination.

I stood up from my chair and walked slowly towards her. Her eyes became wider as I came near her. I went and stood in front of her table.

'Yes' her brother said looking at me. She signalled me to go back to my table from her eyes but I ignored.

'Any problem?' he asked. I still looked in her eyes.

'Actually, I love her' I said.

'What the f...' he said and stood up. Her father now looked at me, keeping his phone aside.

'I really love her sir. I know its funny but I keep thinking about her all the time. I don't do drugs but she has got me really bad. It feels like she's in every part of my blood. Like she's rushing in my body. I love her sir, I really love her' I said as he grabbed me by my collar.

'I am not like other boys sir. I really love her. Though I won't be able to earn much as a writer, I will surely keep her happy. After all happiness can't be bought' I said and she winked.

'Are you sure you will keep her happy?' her father finally spoke.

'Yes sir. I will. Always' I said as he gestured his son to sit down. Mahira stood from her seat and looked at me. It felt like the best feeling ever. I smiled as my heart almost skipped a beat.

'I love you' she said.

'I love you too' I said, closing my eyes, our faces coming closer every second.

'Paneer tikka sir?' I heard a voice.

'Sir?' I heard it again, as a wide smile appeared on my face.

'What?' I said in an angry tone as the waiter stood next to me.

'Do you want me to serve Paneer Tikka sir on your plate sir?' he asked.

'I am non-vegetarian. Go now' I said and clenched my fist as my happy day dream ended. She was still sitting there, eating little bites and occasionally glancing and smiling at me.

'Bastard, you are' Gourav said. I waved my middle finger at his face carefully.

'You didn't tell me where you have been today' he said, eating a mutton kebab slowly. I didn't want him to meet Mahira. I felt a little jealous of his personality as inferiority complex hit me the hardest now.

'I was with her' I said and smiled.

'Her? Who? She? That girl? Wait wait wait. Is she Mahira Bhatt? DAMN' he said and banged his fist on the table.

'Yes. Hey, what the hell is wrong with you?' I asked him.

'You didn't tell me you went on a date!' he said.

'I was going to tell you that' I said, 'now stop being as melodramatic as fuck.'

'Okay. I am sorry. Let's hear it from you' he said.

In the next fifteen minutes forty five seconds (thanks to the stopwatch in my phone), I narrated him with all the details about today. How I thought that I screwed the date by taking up an auto but how love saved us instead. I told him everything.

From everything, I mean everything. How we went to the church together, our little debate on god, our romantic walk on the bridge, wind touching her hair. I was seriously an idiot in love.

'That's so...' he said and paused.

'What? Absurd? Idiotic?' I said trying to fill the empty space he left.

'No. That's so Aww!' he said and I laughed.

'Aww? Like seriously? Where are you learning these words from? Are you...gay?' I said and he frowned. I laughed a little harder.

'Fuck you. I want to meet her. She has done quite some magic over you. Introduce me to her' he said.

'I won't' I said and looked away.

'Why?' he asked.

'You are way too much handsomer than me!' I said and made a face.

'Idiot, you are asshole! That's what love is. Finding imperfections in everyone else and finding perfection in the person you love!' he said and slapped my arm playfully.

'Okay. Let's go' I said and picked up my phone to call Mahira who had finished her dinner by now. She looked at me as her phone rang. I gestured her to meet outside.

'Excuse us' Gourav said as we left the table. I kept holding the stop button from the moment since we stepped into the elevator and waited for her to come.

In two minutes she was there, walking swiftly. She passed a confused look the moment she saw him.

I pressed the ground floor button as the door closed.

'Mahira, this is my cousin Gourav. And Gourav, this is my girlfriend Mahira' I said as he shook hands with her.

'Trust me, I have heard a lot about you' he said as she let out a laugh.

'Seriously?' she said with her eyebrows raised.

'Yes. Mainly praises and shayaries' he said and both of them laughed.

'He's like that only. And I love him' she said as I held her hand, tightly.

'Awwww' Gourav said as both of us laughed again.

'Fuck. I am sorry but my girlfriend has a habit of saying 'Aww' again and again, it has struck in my mind now' he said as he slapped his head.

'Aw. That's so cute' she said. Thank god the person who invented the internet wasn't a woman. Else the link would have started from 'AWWW' instead of 'WWW'.

We stepped out of the lift, talking random shit and laughing together. Gourav recalled his funny incidents with his girlfriend and trust me, they were worth the laughter.

'Ice cream?' I asked her.

'If she's your girl, you don't need to ask. Just take her' he said and winked. She smiled.

'Would you mind to accompany us?' I asked Gourav in the most formal way as possible in front of her. Had she not been there, 'Mother fucker why don't you move that ass' would have been the usual language.

'Me? I thought I would be disturbing you' he said and looked down.

He was now seriously acting like a girl. I laughed.

'Please. Come with us' she said with her eyes gleaming.

'My brother's girlfriend has insisted. How can I turn down the offer now!' he said as we entered the ice cream parlour that was just opposite to the hotel.

'So how come are you here?' I asked her as she looked at the flavours with a child like curiosity.

'I'll have chocolate' she said after a few seconds. The guy nodded.

'We both will have butterscotch' I said as Gourav took out his phone again.

'Actually, dad wanted to talk to bhaiya about his job. He's going to be graduated soon. It's a kind of treat and a discussion, both combined' she said slowly eating the chocolate ice cream from the cup.

Maybe it was the sight of her ice cream laced lips that had now made me sweat. I just wanted to kiss her. I've never kissed ice cream laced lips ever. Well, the truth is that I've never kissed any lips ever. As always, I could do nothing but think about it.

'Thanks to you Mahira, I today know how nature looks like!' he said and she laughed.

'That was really lame. But it was indeed cute. Literally speaking, it was the cutest thing I've ever heard' she said pulling my cheeks.

'I miss Risha. I wish she was here too' he said. Risha had gone out with her family for a trip to Dalhousie.

'Can I see her photo please?' she asked in a childish voice.

'Yes. Why not' he said and opened Skype on his phone.

'Hey baby!' Risha said. It took only two minutes for him to connect the video call.

'Hey. I miss you baby. I love you, come soon please' he said making child like face. He seems stupid.

There's a sea full of irony in the fact that a guy always finds the other guy in love an idiot even though he does talk about the same stupid things to his girlfriend!

'Awww' she said. Gourav was sure to catch this disease.

'Here. Someone's wants to meet you' he said as he handed his phone to Mahira.

'Hi!' she said, with phone in one hand and ice cream in the other.

'Hi! Hey have I seen you before?' she asked confused.

'Um...No. I am Mahira. Sharief's girlfriend' she said and smiled.

'Oh...Mahira! I have heard a lot about you from Sharief. I am a fan. At first I thought that he must be lying, I mean how one can be so much beautiful but now...When I've seen you, he never lied!' she said in an energetic voice.

'That's really nice of you to say that. You are infinite times prettier than me by the way!' she said.

'No. She isn't' I said in reflex.

'I heard it, Sharief' she said. I came near her in order to fit in the frame.

'Aww...You both look perfect! I mean so much cuteness and beauty together! Seriously!' she said.

'Thank you Risha' I said as my phone rang. It was from my dad.

'Where are you two? The dinner has arrived' he said.

'Coming dad. Coming right now' I said and hung up.

Mahira gave the phone back to him as we got out of the parlour and walked into the hotel with ice creams still in our hands.

Gourav was still on Skype with her.

'It's really cute to see them like this. I mean, they are distances apart but still live in each other's heart!' she said, 'hey, did I say something Nobel? I felt like that.'

I laughed pressing the button with 'seventh floor' written on it.

XIX

As the door opened, I saw two familiar figures standing there. One was her brother and the other was her father. My whole body froze, a lump formed in my throat and sweat beads appeared on my forehead.

Fuck! Fuck! Fuck!

Her brother raised an eyebrow the moment he the three of us stepping out of the lift. Only Gourav walked in the most confident way possible. We walked as slow as possible. I wanted time to eat me up so that I could vanish from this horrible situation.

Mahira's face first became expressionless and later struggled for a calm expression. She practised broken fake smiles at them.

'Where have you been?' her brother asked, looking straight into her eyes.

'Uh…' she said and paused. Gourav spoke at that very instant thanks to his reflex situation figuring instincts.

'Sir, actually she owed me an ice cream treat' he said. Her brother still posed confused.

'What?' she muttered as slow as possible.

'Actually sir, I play for the state's Basketball team. Your sister turned out to be a great fan of mine' he said and smiled. Having the physique of hulk, nobody would have ever thought that he was lying.

'I came here just last night. I actually had posted this on Snap chat. She read it and wanted to meet me. She's such a cute girl' he said, his expressions cool as fuck.

'And you…I've seen you somewhere!' he said and rubbed his beard, looking at me.

'I…Sir…' I said as even before I could complete, she spoke.

'He's my friend *bhaiya.* The one from tuition. You have seen him before, right?' she said in the calmest tone possible.

Oh…Yes! You used to be a *takla (bald)*. Grown quite some hair, eh?' he said putting his hand on my shoulder. His touch appeared a little lusty towards me. My girlfriend's brother molesting me, things could only get worse!

I fake smiled. Her father took out his phone and said 'Time *ho gaya hai*'. The three of them stepped in the elevator again as her brother shook hands with Gourav.

'Nice meeting you' he said as the elevator door closed slowly, Mahira blowing me a secret flying kiss which went unnoticed by the others.

'Phewwww' Gourav said a few seconds after the lift moved some floors.

'YOU ARE AMAZING!' I shouted and jumped on him.

'You are so Gay!' he said and laughed. I pulled his cheeks as tightly as possibly. His face looked like made up of metal for the amount of hardness and shine it possessed.

'Stop it. Let me call Mahira and tell her the reality. That her boyfriend who writes Shayaries and all for her is nothing but a gay who's secretly in love with me!' he said, pulling my hand away from his cheeks by his perfect arms.

'Fuck you Gourav. You are so so so so sooo amazing!' I said as the manager of the restaurant came to us provided the level of noise our voices were making, enough to turn most of the heads towards us.

'Is there anything wrong sir?' the manager said with a confused face. He must have thought that we were gay and our affection of love wasn't going well the public.

'Yes sir. He's my brother. Actually we've met after a long time' I lied. He nodded.

'Oh...I see. That's some really good news' he said. We rushed back to the table as fast as possible, later panting after sitting in our seats back.

'Where were you two?' my dad said with anger raging in his tone.

'Ice cream' I said, showing my half eaten cone to him.

'You could have waited. We were going to have it after dinner anyways' he said with his expression colder now.

'Hmm...' I nodded.

The waiter served us with fancy dishes on our plates. Chicken curry, fish, mutton now rested on my plate. I sometimes felt sorry for them. They sacrifice themselves for us. It's what I call 'true love'.

There were numerous discussions taking place on the table. We, the Indians especially middle class have a habit of discussing the most random and the least important subjects sometimes. I mean how on earth 'Has Aishwarya Rai's marriage destroyed her career?' can be a topic to be discussed on the dinner table. Pity on my family.

'She's a nice girl' Gourav said in a low tone, his mouth stuffed with rice.

'I know that, right?' I said and winked.

'You can one day write a novel on her!' he said and I laughed.

'Novel? Like seriously?' I said.

The recent bestsellers have been the tragic ones, in which the either lover dies and many more unrealistic shit. Though I loved reading them, in some part of my mind the question of 'creativity' always arose in my mind.

'Yes' he said and smiled.

'But the ones that are in market right now have tragic ending' I said.

'So what? Give yours a tragic ending too. I will tell her to break up' he said and laughed. I didn't.

'Do you really think she's going to leave an idiot who keeps on thinking about her all the time?' he asked.

'Um…No'

'Then why are you so fucking sad? Break up is a sad reality, bro. No matter how much strong your love is, how many shayaries you write, how many idiotic moons and starts shit you say to your lover; once there is a breakup, it's all over!' he said. 'All over.'

'Would you mind to shut up right now?' I said, almost annoyed.

'I am really sorry. She will really never leave you. You are an idiot and I think she's a bigger one than you!' he said and laughed. His father cleared his throat due to the lack of discipline and table manners the two of us showed.

'Sir would you like to order anything else?' the same waiter who had earlier broken my happy day dream asked.

'Yes. One Paneer Tikka please.'

* * * *

'Okay beta. Bye! Study hard! This is the only year. You already screwed your 10th standard. Take things in a serious way for 12th!' Gourav's father said, putting his hand on my shoulder.

'What?' I said throwing a disappointed look. We were back home after dropping Gourav, his mother and his sisters. His father wanted to talk to my father about some official work so he stayed. Only the two of us sat in the living room.

'Do you have a girlfriend?' he asked.

'Umm...Yes' I replied. His face became the living example of horror.

'What? How? How can you have a girlfriend?' he said in one breath. The level of curiosity in his voice was 'Arnab Goshwami'.

'No. I don't have! Who told you that?' I said in a melodramatic tone.

'You...You said that just now' he said, a little drunk.

'You are a little drunk right now. You should go to your home and sleep' I said standing up and touching his feet. My father, changed into his home clothes just stepped in the living room.

'Good night dad' I said.

'Good night' he said. I vanished into my room and bolted it from inside.

At eleven o'clock my phone rang. It was from an unknown number. I ignored it the first time.

Five minutes later, it rang again. It displayed the same number again. I picked it up.

'Hello' I said half asleep. I was waiting for Mahira to call but she didn't.

'Sharief? Hello. We need you buddy' a familiar voice said from the other side.

'What the f...' I said as the person on the other side cut me mid way.

'Jaskaran here, the editor. I hope you aren't being disturbed' he said. Yes, it was Jaskaran, the editor boy of our school.

Well, I wanted to hung up. First, he never got the things I gave him published in the school magazine. Second, he calls me up whenever he needs some kind of help. In some place of my heart, I was jealous of him too for he was the editor. It was my dream to work as an editor but he snatched the opportunity though I know that he deserved that better than me!

'No...No. Call a half sleepy guy waiting for his girlfriend's call at eleven and he won't be disturbed. No! He surely won't!' I said with sarcasm heavier than Dolly Bindra in my voice.

'Uh...Oh. I am really sorry Sharief but we really need you. Actually it's for the compering' he said.

'Compering for what?' I asked.

'The farewell!' he said in the loudest voice possible. My right ear drum must have been damaged heavily.

'You know I am good at only writing. I can't speak that much good' I said.

'I trust you Sharief. I know you can do this' he said, more motivating than Robin Sharma.

'You think?'

'I believe' he said. I smiled.

'Okay, so I am in' I said.

'We start tomorrow. And hey, how's M?' he asked in a tone that is expected from relatives on result day.

'How do you know about her?' I asked, puzzled.

'That MS in your Instagram's bio. How's she? How did you met her? How did you propose her? God I am dying to hear all this! Not only me, everyone is!' he said.

'What the fuck do you mean by everyone?'

'From everyone I mean the other comperers too! Sana asks me every day about you two' he said.

'I will narrate it all. Now hang up' I said.

'Good night. And hey, tomorrow's 7th February' he said.

Seventh February? What's so special?

'Happy birthday in advance!' I said with the most fakest enthusiasm possible, making the dumbest of the guess.

'No. You are an idiot! Its rose day!' he said.

The biggest dick move in history. 'Valentines week'

'What do I do? Give rose to her?' I asked out of context.

'What else do you want to give?' he said and laughed.

'Bye' I said, my brain almost sleeping now. It felt like a zombie.

'Bye!' he said and hung up.

I jumped from my bed and took out the fifty shades of grey from my book shelf. Well, I wasn't horny at that time but I hid all the money the relatives gave and the pocket money in it.

Valentines week was here and I needed money now. Deep down, I knew that Mahira isn't that kind of girl. The one that gets charmed easily by money or gifts. Still, it was what every guy in relation did. Waste money.

I shook the book and a few five hundred rupee notes fell down on the floor. I collected them and started to count.

Twenty five hundred bucks! Though they are a little less, still I think it will do the magic.

Just a week left for valentines and I still haven't decided what I will gift her.

Chocolates? Books? Dress?

My mind still drowned in the sea named 'confusion' as my phone rang. It was from Mahira.

'Helloooo' she said. She was a little happier than usual.

'Hi love!' I said and smiled. *Love.*

'What's happening? Why haven't you slept till now? You have school tomorrow, right?' she said.

'Yes. But you were going to call and how could I let the love of my life sleep without a smile on her face. Why are you so happy?' I asked. One could easily sense her smile on the other line.

'*Bhaiya* praised about you. Said you look "Shareef" ' she said and chuckled, 'Well, you are Sharief.'

I laughed. The evil guy who called me *takla* (bald) praised me? How's this possible. I would rather believe Adolf Hitler bent on his knees before his girlfriend than this news.

'You know what…' I said.

'What? Tell me! Sounds some good news!' she said in one breath.

'Actually I got an offer for compering in the farewell this year' I said.

'Wohoooo! That's damnsexy news!' she said whistling.

'Uh…I am sorry' she said after a pause.

'Sorry for what?'

'I said 'sexy'. I know you hate it…' she said in a guilty tone as I cut her mid sentence.

'But I love you' I whispered, 'seriously speaking you are the best thing ever happened in my life! My life suddenly transformed from sad to happy then happier and now happiest! You are the only thing God could have gave me at his best! My life is so much fucking better now…All thanks to you…I love you. I really love you! I hope you don't think I am flirting because frankly I suck at flirting' I said.

'Awww…Sharief. I love you too!' she said. I blushed like a fucking idiot.

'You know what's tomorrow?' I asked her.

'Um…No' she said.

'Rose day' I said and she laughed.

'Seriously Sharief? What are we? Eight?' she said and laughed.

'But it would be fun to do all this. Rose day, propose day, chocolate day, teddy day, hug day and….' I said and paused.

'And?' she breathed.

'Kiss day' I said and smiled wide.

'We'll think about it' she said dismissing all the possibilities running in my brain right now about a kiss.

'About what?' I asked acting like I had no idea about what she was talking about.

'The kiss' she said.

'I don't want the Autowalas or that Ayesha to come out of nowhere and destroy our perfect moment!' I said and she laughed hard.

'Am I really just a kiss to you?' she asked.

'Had you been just a kiss to me, I would have rather sent you with Emraan Hashmi movie's DVD's instead of those Shayaries and poems!' I said and there was a brief silence at the line.

'I love you' she said.

'I love you too. Bye' I said.

'Bye!' she said and hung up. I curled up in the bed imagining the endless situations that could be related with a kiss.

I woke up and dressed in my jogging pants. Without telling anyone, I stepped out of the home at five of the morning in search of a rose.

I walked for maybe half an hour until I saw a rose plant. I took out my phone and clicked its picture, sending it to her.

I ran back home and sneaked in my room again. After some workout, I took a shower and got ready for the school.

The class was mostly empty. It sucked to come to school alone. Utsav, Priyanshu, Akshit, Dubey…No one! Traitors!

Thanks heaven I had brought my mobile phone with me. Mahira had took a leave from school today which meant we could talk to each other as much long as we want to. I kept refreshing my Instagram feed to check if she was online or not. She wasn't.

'Mam, Principal Mam is calling Sharief' Jaskaran said as I was in my physics class. Thanks to my physics teacher, she could even teach one student and didn't felt guilty or bored about it. I was juggling with some kinetics numerical at that time.

'You may go' she said resting back in the chair.

'Thank you so fucking much Jaskaran' I said the moment we were out if the class.

'Your welcome. Why is the class empty today? No one except you?' he asked.

'Don't know. How is it going with the compering?' I asked him.

'Here' he handed me a piece of paper with ink splattered on it in random direction.

'What the fuck is this now?' I asked.

'Have a close look at it. It's your script you asshole!' he said. I frowned.

We walked to the principal's office where Sana and Sukriti were waiting for us. Sana was with him and Sukriti was with me. There were two group of comperers. Both of them smiled at me.

'Hi Sharief!' Sukriti said extending her hand towards me.

'Hey!' I said shaking hands gently with her.

'I have been hearing about you' she said and winked.

'Hearing about me?' I said.

'Yes. I have read her all the shayaries you have been posting' Sana said, waving her phone at me with my Instagram's profile open.

'You write really well' Sukriti said, 'that girl is really lucky'.

'I think we are here to meet the principal instead of discussing my love life here' I protested as Jaskaran nodded.

'Actually she's in a meeting. We can sit here' he said pointing towards the sofas in the waiting area.

'Yes. We can' I said and sat on one of the sofa. Sukriti sat next to me and Jaskaran and Sana sat opposite to us.

'So tell me. The story behind 'M&S'' Sana said.

'Yes please' Sukriti said placing her hand just near my shoulder. I felt a little uncomfortable.

'I hope you people have got popcorns with you' I said and started narrating the story till now.

Half an hour later, Jaskaran was burst into claps while the other two girls were now blushing as if Siddarth Malhotra just proposed them.

'Awww....That's so much cute!' Sana said slapping my arm, 'She is Mrs Grey!'

'Mrs Grey?' I asked.

'You proposed her on your birthday because of that Christian Grey and all. So if you are Mr Grey, she is Mrs Grey!' she announced still blushing.

Mrs Grey! Wow! She would be so much happy to hear this!

'You are so romantic. I never expected this. Lucky the girl is' Sukriti said.

My phone vibrated at that moment. It was her call.

'Madam is calling the four of you inside' the peon said from half opened door of the office.

I rejected the call.

"**Laters baby**" I typed and pressed the send button.

XX

The Valentine's week was a mess. With me gifting her small kitkat on chocolate day, my jeans tearing a little apart while proposing her on knees, my inability to afford a teddy bear on Teddy day and so on. Well, she literally loved every part of it. For her, it was the best Valentine's week a girl could ever get and I was the world's best boyfriend for her. We enjoyed every bit of it. Laughing for endless hours, looking at each other and smiling with our hands intervened in one another is something I will never forget in my whole life. Love makes you crazy but happy.

After days of scratching my head, I decided what I will gift her for the valentines. 'Fifty Shades of Grey' for she is Mrs Grey and a pack of chocolates. I was confused as fuck earlier. I fumbled upon Google results which suggested Bouquets and chocolates. I tried asking her indirectly, using the name of Priyanshu's fictional girlfriend but the beauty with a brain she was, she figured it out and said that his girlfriend would want nothing but love. Her little things made me fall in love with her more and more every day, every moment and every second.

As usual, I gave Aryaman the responsibility of getting the chocolates and the book packed. Special instructions that the gift paper should be of red colour, for she loved red was given. He had done his job and the wrapped gift was waiting in my bag, to be delivered to the most beautiful hands in the world soon.

The alarm rang to life and I rubbed my eyes, tapping the snooze button. I checked the wall clock. It was five of the morning.

Today was Kiss day which meant that something could happen today. The possibilities were raised by 200 per cent now. I took off my T-shirt and threw it aside, jumping out of bed for a workout.

After an hour of work out, I picked up my script for the farewell for maybe the nth time. The farewell was tomorrow and Mahira was more excited than me for it. I had read my script to her for maybe more than ten times a day and she had full confidence in me that I'll be the one rocking the stage. Comperers have nothing to rock about. They are just made to be made fun off, abused, hooted and above all, to be thrown tomatoes at!

'Music is life. It is an escape from the mon…' I said and stopped. Fuck the word 'Monotonous', I wasn't able to spell it right even after so much practice.

'Monotonous' her voice rang in my ear, the way she corrected me.

'It's an escape from the monotonous daily boring routine of life. It takes you to places you can never imagine, blah blah blah blah' I said and laughed.

There was a 'Wow' in the script I wasn't able to read properly. It lacked the right feelings for me. I wasn't able to say it properly until she came up with a solution that was laughable but worked!

'Hey, imagine me. Like how do you say 'Wow' when you see me? Try it once' she had said.

I closed my eyes and imagined her.

Dressed in a red top and blue jeans, with light kohl applied on her beautiful eyes and a red lipstick spread on her ever ready kissable lips, she walks towards me slowly and steadily with her eyebrows raised. Those red lips smile the moment they see me.

There's something really good between me and red colour. It's the secret to being turned on for me. I mean I could stare a book in library with a red cover with eyes full of lust, let alone the most beautiful girl in the world dressed in red!

'Wow!' I said in a complete state of amaze, love and a bit of horniness. That sounded perfect.

'Perfect!' she had said and pulled my cheeks. I loved her touch.

After practising again, I threw the script aside and went to the washroom for a shower.

Dressed in my school uniform, I was caught setting my hair in the mirror by my father. He threw his hand in air and then smiled.

'How's the farewell thing going? You can speak well naa?' he asked.

'Of course I can' I said. *Who can't when you have the most beautiful girl in the world by your side?*

He nodded. 'Hurry up.'

'Dad, I have to buy something' I said.

'What?'

'A Nehru jacket'

'And may I ask you why do you want one?'

'It's for the farewell. The teacher has said that boys need to wear a Nehru Jacket with jeans.'

'Okay. We'll go to the mall today. After your tuition' he said and smiled. Why is he smiling so much nowadays?

'Bye dad!' I said and waved at him. I sat in the car, looking at the window struggling to see an image of myself in it.

'School' I said as the driver nodded and stepped his feet on the accelerator.

In half an hour, I was there in the school, thanks to the unnecessary constructions.

I entered the school and saw the preparations for the farewell in the school ground. Little kids dressed in colourful clothes practising their dance performance on a useless song. I smiled at them.

'Hey there! What's up?'Jaskaran said the moment he saw me.

'This shitty thing' I said waving the script at him.

'It's not a shitty thing' he said and frowned, 'I've wrote my heart out.'

'Using heavy words to fool the audience is called 'writing your heart out', haan?' I said.

'Please' he said, 'I hope you have practised well. Principal's going to hear us today.'

'I have practised well! Guess who helped me with this?' I said with a smile.

'Miss Bhatt' he said and I blushed, 'she has done quite some magic over you hasn't she?'

'Yes' I said. *She is the best magician in the world. She turns a horror movie into a romantic one, can make my heart beat faster, can make me feel I am on drugs and much more. She indeed has a superpower named 'Love'.*

'Hey guys!' Sana said. We high fived her.

'Mr Grey. I hope you have worked on that expressionless 'wow' of yours' she said.

'Mrs Grey helped me with it' I said with a hint of pride in my smile. I was proud of her; I wanted to scream this in each and every year on earth!

'May I see the improved version of your 'wow'? The one 'MRS GREY' taught you?' she said, laying stress on 'Mrs Grey'.

I closed my eyes again, a little softly this time and imagined her again. Dressed in the same clothes, wearing the same lipstick, coming downstairs from her home, her little hair bouncing with every step she took. Those kohl eyes hunted me. I grinned and said 'wow'.

'BASTARD!' she said and slapped my arm hard.

'What?' I asked with innocence dropping from every alphabet.

'I know what you were thinking! Pervert! All the boys are the same!' she said and laughed.

'When did you try all the boys?' I said and she frowned.

'Shut up. You are so pervert' she said and grinned.

'Okay. I am. There's only one thing in our mind all the time' I said.

'Hmm...' she said and laughed again.

'I am talking about cricket, you cheap thinker' I said. Both of us burst into laughter.

'Haan...what were you talking about?'Jaskaran said looking up from his script. He was lost in that god damn script of his all the time like both of us never existed. He was serious about his job, being the 'editor'. Had I been the editor, I would have smoked weed and waved my middle finger at the guys who threw him with so much of work.

'I am tensed and fucking nervous right now' he said, wiping sweat beads off his forehead.

'There's nothing to be tensed about' Sana said, putting her hand on his shoulder.

'Where is Sukriti?' I asked. Both of them pouted.

'What the? Where is she?' I said, a little angry this time.

'Studying, in her class. Said she can't go to meet the principal as she has some important assignment to do' Jaskaran said.

'I am a medical student. You two are non-medical and she is commerce. How the fuck on earth is a commerce student supposed to have more work than science students?' I said, more of barked.

'She must be in her class. Go and ask her!' Sana said. I nodded and left for her class.

I knocked at the door to check if there was a teacher inside. There wasn't. The door was slightly open. I knocked it again. No response again.

Three more knocks later, I slam opened the door and saw Sukriti sitting with her boyfriend, hand in hand, both of them looking at me as if I was nude and my modesty was visible.

'I am sorry. Really sorry' I said as I waved my hand in air and left the class. Jaskaran blew me a flying kiss from the other corner of the corridor. I waved my middle finger at him.

'We have to go' he said, showing me his watch.

'I am not going inside again. Sana will go' I said, 'you knew she was with him. Why did you sent me? I am already missing Mahira' I said and frowned. Both of them made puppy faces.

'Aw…So cute' they said in unison and then burst into laughter.

'Fuck your cuteness. Let's go now' I said as I started to walk.

Yes, I was nervous. The last time we met the principal, she declined to hear us as she found a hell lot of grammatical errors in our script. She gave us a week for us to do all the corrections and come to her prepared. I wanted to escape right now, somewhere I couldn't be found. I know that my pronunciations suck big time. Thanks to auto correct, I was able to get the spelling of 'pronunciations' right.

I took out my phone as we sat in the waiting area again. I opened 'IMO' and video called Mahira. After four rings, she picked it up.

'Someone's looking really cute today!' she said the moment my ugly face appeared in front of her. The rest three giggled as they heard it.

She was sitting in her bed, wearing a blue T-shirt that had white lining on it. I smiled the moment when her face appeared on the screen.

'I am not looking cute. I am fucked up. Big time' I said.

'So what? Everyone's fucked up big time. There's no issue to it' she said, 'you are really looking sooo cute today. What's the fun of so much technology when you can't even pull the cheeks of someone through the internet? Huh' she frowned.

'I have to speak in front of the principal. She's like sitting inside with a belt in her hand. I am going to go inside, remove my pants and let her hit my butt' I said as I took out my handkerchief to shoo away the mosquitoes buzzing near me. Thanks to the school authority, those who pay the fees are made to sit under a fan and those who take the fees are made to sit under air-conditioner.

'You have practised your lines enough times. You speak so well. Don't take so much stress' she said.

'Yes. I don't think I should be over thinking this. What's the worse they can do? Throw me out? As if I was dying to be a part of this' I snapped, angrily.

'This is the reason why I don't like talking to you sometimes. You get angry at little things. Why are you like this?' she frowned.

Uh…I am sorry. I won't be angry again' I said. Her face still the same.

'You say this every time that you won't be angry and what happens later? You end up breaking a skull or two' she said, avoiding eye contact.

'I am sorry. Really sorry' I said.

'Serious?'

'Yes. I promise there's nothing like anger in my life from now' I said. Her face brightened up.

'That sounds good now' she said and smiled.

'Remember what day it is today?' I asked her, suppressing a smile.

'Friday' she said and passed an *I know what you mean but still I am a girl and girls are innocent* smile.

'Kiss day' I said and grinned like an idiot as numerous situations and possibilities of a kiss exploded in my mind at that very moment.

'Oh…' she said and laughed.

'No 'Oh'. Only 'Muahh'' I said, pouting in the camera. I heard giggles and startled as I saw all the rest of the three staring at me.

'We'll think about it' she said.

'Stop acting like my dad. Tell me. Yes or no' I said. I couldn't wait anymore to kiss the world's most perfect lips now. I shifted in my seat as the thought ran a chill down my spine.

'Um…I told you we'll think about it' she said trying hard to suppress a smile. Her words tried hard but her dimples gave it all away

'I have to give something to you. Don't miss the class today' I said.

'The only thing I miss is you' she said. I laughed hard.

'What?' she said, her expressions confused as ever.

'Miss Bhatt, I feel it's my responsibility to tell you that you tried to become romantic just a moment ago but failed miserably' I said. She frowned.

'I am no writer naa. That's why' she said. I smiled.

'Madam is calling you inside' the same peon said, through the door.

'Got to go' I said to her.

'Bye! Rock it!' she said as she passed a flying kiss. I smiled and switched off my phone.

'Madam can we come in' I said, holding the door of her room. The temperature in her room could even put both the North and

South Pole to shame. I wanted to curse her for she made us wait in buzzing mosquitoes while she herself was busy discussing ways to screw the parents more in her air-conditioned room.

'Good morning madam' I said. She nodded, her eyes still on the file on her table.

'Please have a seat' she said. She was acting generously.

'I am Sharief Malhotra and this is my partner Sukriti' I said. She smiled.

'I am Jaskaran, madam. The editor and this is my partner Sana' he said. She smiled and nodded.

'I hope you have done all the corrections necessary' she said.

'Yes madam, we have. Shall we start it now?' Jaskaran said.

'Yes please' she said as all of us stood from our chairs and started reading our parts one by one.

I don't know what it was, maybe her voice, her smile or the flying kiss she blew in the end that kept me from stumbling in between. I read my lines in full confidence and that 'wow' was almost breath taking though it took me twenty four seconds to imagine her.

'That was really good!' the principal said as Sana said the last line of her script. She stood from her chair and passed us smiles. She was impressed.

'Thank you, madam. Thank you so much' I said as all of us thanked her.

'Best of luck for tomorrow!' she said with her extra brilliant smile.

'Thanks again mam' Jaskaran said as we left the office with a smile.

'Wohoo!' Sana said, 'we are finally ready!'

'Of course we are' I said, smiling.

'All thanks to Mrs Grey' Jaskaran said as the three of them chuckled.

'Can I see her sometime?' Sukriti asked, her face puppy like.

'Yes. You can.'

'Cheers!' Jaskaran said taking out a diet coke can from his back pocket.

'If that can is from inside your ass, I better stay away from it' I said and everyone burst into laughter.

I took out my phone and tried calling her. She didn't pick. I tried three more times. No answer.

After the final rehearsals, we wished each other best of lucks and discussed the dress code. The boys were wearing Nehru Jackets while the girls were wearing Sarees. This dress code was decided after a long debate that lasted for more than two hours. Thanks to Rovio, I had Angry birds with myself to stay away from the shitty discussion.

As I sat in the car, I took out my phone again and tried calling her. Her phone was now switched off. I tried calling her alternate number and to my surprise, it came as Not Reachable.

Was it the kiss thing that was eating her up?

Okay, so frankly speaking I have never kissed anyone. I have no experience of kissing. This doesn't means that I am craving for a kiss or all I want from her, like all the other boys want from their girlfriends, is a kiss. No. Kiss, for me is a step to take relation forward. I think I have fucked up with the kiss thing. I shouldn't have told her that. Though she sounded happy, I have a gut feeling that I have screwed up big time.

After a few more unsuccessful tries, I stopped calling her. I decided that whatever I have to tell her about the whole 'Kiss' thing, I'll be telling her face to face. Moreover, I had to give her Valentine's gift. Just two more hours and we'll meet. I will surely try to fix any misunderstanding.

In another half hour we were home. I quickly changed into fresh clothes and sat in the living room waiting for the clock to hit 4:00. My mother offered me lunch, which I declined lying that I had something at school. The fact that something was not good between me and Mahira was eating me every second now. I tried to call her again but her phone was still switched off.

The moment the clock hit 4:00. I jumped from the sofa and went to my room to take her gift with myself. I glanced at the two red boxes again. One had the book, the other had the chocolates. I touched them sweetly and imagined her reaction.

'Wow' No she won't say something like this.

'This wasn't needed' Maybe.

'I love you so much for this!' Nah. Out of the list. She never craves for gifts.

The kind of girl she was, I feared that she would throw the gifts back at me. The present situation made it even worse.

I stuffed two Spray Mints in my pocket for the case of emergency and sat in the car.

There was a huge traffic jam on the Tawi Bridge. Way too huge. People honked unnecessarily. Butterflies flew in my stomach. I couldn't wait anymore.

'Can I walk from here?' I asked the driver.

'Walk? It's some twenty minutes more from here' he said as he adjusted the mirror.

I looked at my watch. It showed 4:17. I had to reach there before 4:40. Staying in the car meant being struck in the traffic for some forty or fifty minutes more. It was now or never.

'Bye bhaiya. I am getting late. I'll go by my own' I said as I got out of the car and slammed the door shut before he could even say something.

I ran. The last time I remember running so much faster was in seventh standard when my neighbour's German shepherd had gone frenzy. I ran as fast as I could. I smiled as I saw the place where the both of us stood, on the bridge on our first date. The memories of her hair flying and our hands intervened with each other hit me hard. I grinned like an idiot and ran even faster.

It took me eighteen minutes to reach the main building of our tuition. I was exhausted completely, with my tongue outside my mouth and my whole body drenched in sweat. My hairs were ruffle now I felt limbless. My voice was now hoarse as every part of my mouth craved for water.

As I entered the building, my worst nightmare came true. After twenty minutes of hard running, I enter the main building of the tuition just to see that the elevators were not working. I cursed loudly in air and climbed the stairs as fast as I could. By the time I reached the third floor, I felt I would now just die.

My lungs exploded and my heart beat was unusual.

'Medical' I asked the receptionist the moment I entered the room

'What?' the receptionist said, rather in shock. I looked like a rape victim who just ran from the people who had captivated her.

'Which room? 11th Medical?' I barely managed to speak.

'Room number three. And have this' she said passing a water bottle to me. The exhausted muscles of my face barely managed to smile.

I gulped down the whole water down at once while running to the room number three. The asshole I was, I tripped down just before entering the room. I stood and slammed open the door.

'What the f…' I said with my mouth barely open. It was 4:40 and the class hadn't started yet. There were only four people sitting in the class. Utsav, Ayesha, Isha and Karan.

'Everything alright?'Utsav asked me as I sat down.

'M…Mahira…Where…Is…She?' I said, breathing heavily.

'She won't come today' Isha said looking at me.

'Wha…' I said and fell on the desk, completely exhausted hitting the wall.

'Sharief!'Ayesha said, coming towards me.

'Why…Isn't she here?…Her…Phone…switched…off' my tongue flapped producing sounds.

'It's her brother' Isha said.

'Her brother?' I asked, coming back to my senses now.

'The fuck!' I said cursing as loud as possible.

'Her brother has got to know everything about us. All three of us. Me, Mahira and Ayesha. He has warned her now' she said.

'Warned? As in.'

'Stay away from you' she said as my heart completely stopped.

'It's not a problem. She said she'll find a way to work it out' she continued as her last sentence acted as a CPR for me. My heart beat was normal now.

'But her brother himself has a girlfriend! So much fakeness I tell you' I said and managed to laugh.

'Shut up. She said she's sorry for not coming today' she said and smiled. I could imagine her puppy sorry face. I grinned.

'Here' I said taking out the two boxes wrapped in red out of my bag, 'give these to her. On Sunday.'

'Aye Aye captain' she said and laughed.

The sir entered the moment and started to teach the five students in the class. I missed her badly.

* * * *

'This colour will do it' my mother said as she handed me a blue Nehru jacket. We were in Lifestyle, Wave mall.

'Hurry up' my father said as he was on his phone, checking his mail. Gourav was talking to his girlfriend.

'Try this' she said handing me another blue Nehru jacket.

'These are all blue maa. What's wrong with you?.'

'This is dark blue, this is light blue and this, and it is navy blue' she said. My head which was already puzzled tried to avoid being caught in a fight with her.

'Maa please' I said. I gestured Gourav.

'What?' he said putting his phone in his pocket.

'Take this' I said handing a thousand rupee note to him.

'What do you think am I? A prostitute?' he said.

'Fuck you' I said as slow as possible while my mom selected different shades of blue, 'get me four tickets of Sanam Re.'

He let out a laughter. My mother startled and looked at him, shockingly.

'Are you serious? Not Deadpool but Sanam re?'

'Shut the fuck up and do what I said' I said. He frowned.

'Can I ask you something?' he said, scratching his head, his biceps barely struggling in the white T-shirt.

'Yes, you can buy one of the 'Deadpool' for you' I said as he smiled. He loved when someone gave him a movie treat.

'But why four? Not two?'

'Privacy *naam ki cheez suni hai tune?*' (ever heard of something called 'Privacy'?).

He nodded and disappeared. I took out my phone and dialled her number again. It was still switched off.

'This is perfect' my mother said, finally after half an hour.

'Isn't it the same one you first selected and later kept aside?' I asked.

'Shut up' she said.

After buying me the Nehru Jacket, the five of us went for a dinner. I tried calling her again and again, checked if she was online but nothing was successful.

The dinner was ordered and it arrived on our table. My mind still roamed here and there with Isha's words ringing in my ears.

It's her brother

Suddenly my phone rang. It was an unknown number.

'Sharief' I said. There was no sound at the other side other than that of heavy breathing.

'Hello?' I said again.

'H...Hello Shar...ief' a female voice said. I smiled wider than ever when I heard that voice. It was her.

'Excuse me' I said to my parents as Gourav threw me a confused look. I got out of the restaurant to attend her call.

'Where have you been?' I asked her, 'Why the fuck is your phone switched off? Why didn't you come today? I had told you I want to give you something' I bombarded her with questions.

There was no answer from the other side. Not even to one of the questions.

'I...I...am sorry' she said, her voice broken.

'Sorry for what?' I said, confused.

'I don't think I can continue with the relation' she said as I was about to drop my mobile.

'What...What are you saying?' I said, tears emerging out of nowhere in my eyes. *Yes, boys who love cry.*

'I am really sorry' she said, 'I love you but I can't carry with the relation anymore.'

'What happened? At least tell me' I said.

'It's my brother, Sharief. He has got to know everything about us' she said with little sobs in between.

'So what? We didn't have…' I was about to say as she cut me mid way.

'He said "Parents give freedom. That doesn't means that you'll misuse it" He told me some things which have now completely shattered me!' she said.

I wanted to go to her home and fight with that evil bastard. Gourav was infinite times more powerful than him and he could knock him down in one punch.

'I am sorry…You are not wrong but neither he is…' she said, 'I love you…'

'Why are you doing this to me?' I asked her, now almost crying. I wanted my mom to slap me awake and tell me that this was a bad dream. A bad fucking dream.

'I am doing nothing, Sharief…It's the time that is doing everything' she said. She was now crying too.

'I am sorry…Really sorry…I hope you understand' she said.

I wanted to yell at her and abuse her but my lips couldn't. I loved her. I could never even think like that.

'I…understand' I said. There was no response from the other side. Just sobbing noises.

'Why can't we be together? Why is it only me who gets fucked every time?' I spat on the floor, sulking as a tear rolled down my cheek…

'I…. am sorry Sharief. I can't go against him. He's my brother.'

'I…Love you' I said.

'I love you too sha…' she said as I felt stabbed in the back. She was lying. She never loved me. Yes, she never did. She's a liar.

'Good bye' I cut her and hung up.

My eyes burnt, as I clenched my fist. I wanted to knock her brother down now but I couldn't. After all he was a brother. He was right in his own way.

I sat aside and looked at her picture in my phone. Some drops appeared on my phone's screen from nowhere. I looked up to see if it was the rain. It wasn't the rain, it was the 'pain' that was making me cry. I cried endlessly, hugging my phone hard.

One could have easily mistaken me as a person who lost his loved one in an accident just now. My mind now was completely shattered. My face muscles twitched.

I loved her so much and what did she do? Fuck me up? Leave me?

'What happened?' Gourav said, as he came out looking for me.

'Nothing' I said wiping tears from my T-shirt, 'Nothing.'

From chicken to the dessert, everything went untouched that evening. The tickets were sprayed with a perfume and burnt with a matchstick. I clenched the burning tickets in my hand. The fire was nothing compared to the one burning inside me.

It's funny how the person on whom you wasted more than six months of your life, thinking, and caring, loving, writing about didn't even bother to waste six minutes of her life to think once again before breaking up.

The fact that you survived so many years before meeting that person but after they come in your life and leave, even surviving a day seems impossible, has always drawn middle fingers to the emotion called 'Love.'

XXI

'What happened?' Gourav whispered in my ear for the sixth time. We were sitting in the living room, watching 'Two States'. His family had come for a night stay. My father chatted endlessly with his, my mother gossiping about Sharma ji's daughter who had three affairs at a time and my sister discussing nail paint colours with his sisters. The TV was just turned on for the sake of formality. I stared the TV blankly.

He kept pushing me to tell him what had happened. I declined. I was busy in watching the movie or should I say, distract myself from whatever had happened.

My heart pained at the scene where the girl leaves the boy for her family. Girls are like this only. Mahira is no different.

Make up and Break up, the two pastimes of girls!

'For god sake Sharief, tell me what happened? Else I am going to Mahira's home!' he said, a little louder this time.

'Go!' I shouted as all heads turned towards me.

'Mother f...' he mumbled and stood up.

'Where are you going now?' his father asked him.

'To have some fresh air' he said and rolled his eyes. He climbed the stairs and disappeared.

'Carry on everyone' I said as everyone went back in their own world of discussions. I picked up the remote and raised the volume to the max.

I loved her. I still do. Why did she do this to me?

'You are an asshole. An ugly one' my idiotic side said and laughed an evil laughter.

'See his face. He's evil. There must have been some problem, that's why she left you. Stop acting like an idiot now. You need to sleep. It's one already. You have to host that god damn Farewell tomorrow' the intelligent side said.

'Yes, there is a problem. You. See yourself. How much ugly, useless, talentless and unromantic son of a bitch you are. Who the fuck gives a fifty bucks 'KitKat' on chocolate day? Hahaha' the idiotic side said and laughed again.

'Don't listen to him. I say again, don't. Sleep.'

'No. Don't sleep. You should cry. Grab a drink, call her and curse the living shit out of her. She deserves this. And those motherfucking gifts you got for her, what about them?'

'I tell you. Sleep and give your best tomorrow! She'll be so happy' the intelligent side said.

'FUCK YOU. SHE SCREWED YOU. SCREWED. BOLD AND CAPITAL LETTERS! THAT TICKETS YOU BURN'T, ALL THE MONEY YOU WASTED, AND WHY DOES THIS HAPPENS ONLY TO YOU? FIRST MOHINI AND NOW HER. THE SIMPLEST REASON IS THAT YOU ARE AN IDIOT. I-D-I-O-T' the idiotic side shouted, almost damaging my ear drums.

I shook my head. Yes, first Mohini and now Mahira. Girls whose names start with 'M' have the moral right to screw me. They have the permission from God.

I stood up and unplugged the TV from the socket. There was an awkward silence for a few seconds.

'I have to go to the Farewell tomorrow. Going to sleep. Good night' I said to everyone and went in my room, bolting it from inside.

I had switched off my phone and vowed not to turn it to power. Changing into the home clothes, I threw my phone on the bed.

I removed the wall clock from the wall and kept it on the bed. Hugging the clock tight, I tried hard to sleep but couldn't.

'The only thing I miss is you' her words ringed in my ears.

'I love you' she had said. That smile with those dimples appeared in my mind.

'We'll go somewhere where money can't afford happiness. Where we could be happy without sipping over priced coffees and sitting in air-conditioned cafes' her words repeated in my brain.

'FUCK!' I shouted and threw the wall clock aside. It shattered into pieces. The glass was now lying in million pieces in the other corner of the room. Still, those pieces were less than those of my broken heart right now.

The whole night passed in sulking and crying. It felt like someone had accidentally spilled water on my bed. It was all wet, with my tears. I was being a cry baby but I had no control over myself.

Had forgetting people completely from our mind been as easy as forgetting wifi networks for a mobile phone, life would have been much easier.

I heard a knock at the door. I took a towel and wrapped it around my face, to avoid my red eyes being exposed.

'Who is that?' I asked. There was no response.

I opened the door to see Gourav standing there, in his night clothes, rubbing his eyes.

'Good morning. I thought of giving you a friendly reminder that your farewell function starts in an hour' he said as I startled.

'Fuck' I said, 'I should have been dressed by now.'

'Yes. Your welcome' he said, with his face calm and left. He was behaving a little absurdly.

I took a shower, brushed and got dressed in thirty minutes. I looked at myself in the mirror. Dressed in Blue Nehru Jacket and blue jeans, my face was still down with my eyes swollen red.

'Someone's looking really cute' I heard from behind. I turned and saw no one. I shook my head and smiled.

I picked up my phone and put it in my pocket. I practised fake forceful smiles in the mirror. I didn't want to look like a guy who just got his first breakup. Breakup from a girl he loved so much, he kept thinking about her each and every moment of his life. I failed miserably and I had started to forget my lines. I picked up the script and glanced at it. It looked completely alien now as I wasn't even able to recall a single line from it.

'I am waiting for you in the car' Gourav said and disappeared. I nodded and held the script in my hands.

I sat in the car with the script in my hand, staring blankly at it.

'I am asking you for the last time. Will you tell me what happened?' Gourav said, annoyed.

I didn't respond. Just turned the FM radio on. It played 'Main Dhoondne ko Zamaane Main' that matched my situation in one way or the other.

'Okay. Don't tell me' he said and stepped his feet on the accelerator.

The car came to a screeching halt after fifteen minutes at my school's gate.

'Best of luck' he said as I stepped out. I passed him a fake smile.

'Thank you' I said, softly closing the door. He drove away.

I entered the school with millions of things running in my mind. The security guards didn't receive my salute that day.

The maids weren't greeted with my 'Namaste' like every day since the past eight years I've been in the school. Anyone could have figured out that I wasn't okay.

'Mr Grey *aa gaye*' Sana said. (Mr Grey is here). I didn't reply.

'You are looking good today' Sukriti said. She was dressed in a black T-shirt and red jacket with black jeans.

'Thank you. You look beautiful too' I said and fake smiled. Every girl, except my mother and sissies now burnt my blood. All of them are the same. Fool idiot guys like me, enjoy, make them crazy about you and later, leave them.

'What's wrong?' Sana said putting her hand on my shoulder.

'Um…Nothing' I said in the most fakest tone possible.

'You don't look okay' she said.

'Yes…I've had a fight with Mahira' I said.

'Aw…Such a lover you are, one fight and you are so sad. It's all going to be okay' she said. Jaskaran nodded his eyes still on his script.

I wanted to shout at her that I had a god damn breakup and it's never going to be okay again. It's easy to say that everything is going to be okay but only the guy who gets his balls squeezed in all this knows the pain!

'Sharief…Mohini wanted to talk to you' I heard a familiar voice from behind and felt a pat on my shoulder.

It was Dhananjay. I hugged him tight.

'I know whatever happened. It's going to be all right, okay?' he said.

I scratched my head.

'Who told you?' I asked him, confused.

'Haha! We've seen each other's dicks and here you are, hiding things from your brother' he said and laughed.

I hugged him more tightly as tears again appeared in my eyes. It was enough crying now. I didn't want to cry anymore.

He rubbed my head.

'It's going to be all right! Everything's going to be okay' he said, 'Mohini was looking for you.'

'As if five years of fucking wasn't enough for her. What does she wants?' I asked him.

'Don't know. She said she wants to say something to you and also wants you to meet someone' he said.

'Meet who?'

'I don't know naa. She's there, in the props stall. Go' he said.

I was in no mood to even see her face, let alone the thing of talking to her. She was the first girl to fuck me so badly and later, Mahira did the same. Kind of the same.

I walked slowly to the props stall. My old friends from 10th standard waved at me. I kept passing fake smiles.

Mohini was dressed in black top and black jeans. She was busy with some work of hers, with hairpin in her mouth. She was standing on her toes and adjusting some prop. I went near her and greeted her in the most fakest tone possible.

'Hi there friend!' I said with fake enthusiasm. Her blue eyes became big the moment she saw me and her face lit up.

'Finally' she said, 'I want to say so many things to you.'

'I am dying to hear it all' I said. **Bitch I have no fucking interest in listening you** could have been a better response.

'But first…I want you to meet someone' she said.

Meet who? Umaan?

'Who do you want me to meet now?' I said, annoyed. I looked at my watch. Half an hour more for the programme to start.

'He has gone to the restroom. He'll be here soon…Um…Here he is' she said pointing behind me. I turned around and saw the mother fucker I hated the most on earth. Diveesh.

He was dressed in a blue T-shirt with parallel jeans. He looked a bit taller than the last time I had seen him, though he still was a short cheap asshole. He smiled his fucking fake smile at me.

Anger rushed through my veins at that moment. I never wanted to come across him, ever in my life because I wanted to beat the living shit out of him. I was bad at anger. Still, the guts of this guy, he came to meet me, the guy whom he fucked with his cheap tantrums.

'Hi!' he said. I clenched my fist hard and bit my tongue as I was going to abuse him.

'The fuck are you doing here!' I shouted angrily.

'Easy bro, easy' he said as he kept his hand on my shoulder.

'NO…Get your fucking cheap hand off me' I said, removing his hand from me with full force.

'I know I have done wrong. I am sorry' he said.

'And I was wrong too. I misunderstood you, Sharief. I am sorry' Mohini said.

'What the fuck is happening here? I don't want you two to show your acting skills here' I said and started to walk away.

Mohini held my hand. It was the first time I had a physical contact with her.

'Please…Sharief…We are sorry' she said.

'So was this all planned? 'WE' are sorry. You two planned to fuck me up?' I barked.

'It was entirely my mistake' he said, looking down, 'I lied to her.'

'And my mistake was to trust him. I believed him. I let you down, Sharief. I am sorry. Both of us are. I miss us, our moments.

The moments we spent together, playing, studying, and gossiping. I miss our friendship' she said. Her words felt like a knock to my already *in pain* head.

'Can we forget everything that happened?' Diveesh spoke.

'We can't. No, we can't. I loved you so much and this, this mother fucker standing right here took you away from me! In one moment' I said.

'He is sorry' she said, 'so am I.'

'I am really sorry, Sharief. Please. Understand' he said.

'You should give them a second chance!' my intelligent side said.

'Fuck them up! Fuck them! They are the same as Mahira' the idiot shouted.

'It's all up to you, Sharief. You have committed mistakes in your life too and you very well know how much it hurts when someone doesn't accept your apology' the intelligent side said.

'Only if you two are not acting, it's okay' I said as a drop of tear ran down her cheek. She came near to hug me but I stepped aside.

'I am sorry…bro…Really' he said, hugging me tight. His short frame just reached my shoulders.

'I've heard you are going to be the host. I'll be the one whistling and clapping for you the first!' he said with enthusiasm. He ran his hand through his pockets.

'I'll cheer for you' Mohini said with her smile.

'Fuck! I left my phone home. Sharief, I need to make a call. Can you please give me yours?' he said.

'Um…Here' I took it out from my pocket and handed him, 'It's switched off right now. You'll have to power it on.'

'Okay' he said. Suddenly there was a voice from the stage mic.

'Sharief Malhotra, Sukriti Mahajan, Jaskaran Gujral and Sana Dubey are requested to come on stage. Right now' the teacher announced.

'Got to go' I said to Mohini. Diveesh was still on the phone, calling someone. He gave me thumbs up before I left.

I hastily climbed the stairs of the stage and stood on the podium. I kept my script aside and waited for Sukriti to come. In five minutes, she was there.

'All set?' she asked me.

'Yes' I said. She adjusted her hair. The crowd settled down as the principal and the chief guest walked slowly towards their seats.

'Start it now' she said. I kept staring the crowd blankly and saw Diveesh and Mohini sitting together, waving towards me. Diveesh clicked pictures from my mobile.

'Good morning to all the students, Principal mam and the chief guest, Mr Balwinder, Honb'le MLA of the state' I said.

'All of you are idiot. Yes, all of you. You are the biggest one. Can't you see that I had a fucking breakup? No you can't. You want me to kiss this idiot's ass with words dipped in honey when the reality is that he is a thief! A fucking thief! Why is it only me all the time, all of you want to screw, huh? There are seven billion people on earth. Why Sharief Malhotra does gets fucked all the time. What am I? A fucking joker. Yes, a joker. Joker makes you laugh, makes you smile and what not. But the thing that Joker isn't capable is of making you fall in love with him. I am a joker. Though I have not painted my face up or have a red nose that 'PINGS' whenever pressed, I have this face. This ugly face that nobody likes. This is why Mohini screwed me. This is why Mahira did the same' I paused. The face of the Principal turned pale and the chief guest took out his phone and acted like he didn't listen it all. The teacher took out their handkerchief and starts to wipe sweat off their faces. I expected tomatoes anytime now.

'I am UGLY, poor; I don't have a body that was built in gym. But this doesn't means that I am a time pass or my feelings have no value. I am not woody, from the Toy Story with whom you play for some time and throw it away. I am a fucking human. I have feelings but...My feelings have no value because I am ugly. I don't have muscles to flaunt, I don't have a limousine but I surely have a heart. There was a girl, I thought who loved me. I thought she was the one who saw my heart but no...she was the same. She left me for her brother. She is right;it's her brother that should matter more to her. After all, It's been six months that I have been with her but her brother is since she was even born...But the thing she failed to realise was that I loved her. I still do. Maybe not more than her brother but I do. I care for her. I think of her, I have written endless shayaries about her. Want to know the funny fact? She just called me and said 'I AM SORRY'. Hahaha! Sorry? For breaking me? For not valuing my feelings? She doesn't need to be sorry at all. I am a joker. I trip, I cough, and I die to make people laugh. Nobody needs to apologize to me' I said as the crowd hooted furiously and the Principal stepped up from her seat and looked at me with her eyes wide.

'I don't want to speak in front of you fake people anymore. Bye bye fake people!' I said and started walking away from the stage.

I felt a pinch at my back.

'Music embarks a blissful journey...speak...Music embarks a blissful journey' Sukriti said as low as possible. The crowd looked at my blank face. The principal smiled at me and the chief guest nodded, as if gesturing me to speak.

'Music...embarks...a...blissful...journey...Should I speak your lines?' she said slowly, her mouth away from the mic.

'Music embarks a blissful journey...it takes you to places you can't describe. Away from the boring routine...' I started to speak from my script and thanked god for the deadly day dream he just gave me.

The function took place normally. The crowd didn't hoot neither did the chief guest walked away. I was still recovering from the trauma that the day dream just gave me.

The cultural programme ended with a classical dance performance. The crowd clapped and ran towards the food stall. Akshit sang in his lovely and seductive voice while Priyanshu displayed his Guitar skills. Something he knows other than fantasizing about food or acting like a self styled relationship expert.

I went to Mohini and Diveesh. Both of them looked pretty impressed with my performance.

'That was really nice!' she said.

'Thank you' I said with a broken smile.

'Let's celebrate somewhere! Let's go!' Diveesh said. I rolled my eyes at him.

'Please....Sharief.' Mohini said with her puppy like face.

'Okay. But where do we go?' I asked.

'Somewhere fun' Diveesh said and giggled. I rolled my eyes again. I checked my watch; it was five of the evening.

'To the parking lot' he said. We started walking towards the lot. He took out the key of his new SUV and clicked the button. The lights were on.

'You two, sit behind' he said.

'I can sit with you' I said opening the door next to the driver's seat.

'No. Sit with her, sir' he said, sitting in the driver's seat. Mohini dragged me behind and made me to sit with her.

'Okay guys, let's go!' he shouted pressing the music player's button. It played a party song.

He drove fast through the lanes. He kept honking, singing the songs loud as the volume was at the max. Mohini was lost in the music too. She kept shouting the lyrics and grooving a little in her seat.

'You are a bitch' I murmured as slow as possible.

'What?' she said, her hand behind her ear, 'I can't hear you.'

'Saying the lyrics of the song' I said. She nodded.

The car came to a screeching halt in front of a liquor shop. Diveesh turned the music player off and smiled.

'Show time' he said and got out of the car, disappearing in the shop.

'I don't drink' I said. Mohini made a face.

'You are so uncle types. You'll have to' she said and pulled my cheek. The cheek pull reminded me of Mahira. I wanted to slap Mohini now.

'Take this guys' Diveesh said, handing a short bottle to both of us, one in his own hand.

'What's this?' I asked.

'Rum' he said, 'you'll have to drink' he removed the cap from his bottle and started drinking it. He gulped down it all in three sips.

Mohini started drinking too. I made a face.

'Drink!' she said.

I removed the cap slowly and brought the bottle close to my mouth. The smell wasn't good at all.

'Like this' she said and forced the bottle in my mouth. I coughed some of it out. It tasted sweet and spicy at the same time. It burnt my tongue.

'Ahem…ahem' I splattered some of it out.

'Uh…oh' she said and started wiping it off my jeans with her handkerchief. Her touch was seductive.

'Be slow' Diveesh said, 'Lets go now' he stepped his feet on the accelerator.

He kept driving like hell, listening to party songs and cursing everyone. For three hours. It was eight thirty and everything was dark now. He stopped the car near the church. The same church I and Mahira had gone on the date for the first time.

'I have some work. Will be here soon. Till then, you guys can talk' he said, getting out of the car and disappearing in the dark. The road was empty and the street light flickered.

There was an awkward silence between me and her. I stared the gate of the church as my mind replayed every moment of our date. Tears appeared in my eyes. In few more moments, I was crying. My head was paining now as the Rum had started to show its effect.

'Why are you crying?' she asked coming near me, holding my head, 'I am sorry for whatever I did to you.'

'Okay. It's okay' I said.

'He lied to me' she said.

'He didn't lie. He said the truth. You are sexy' I said, my tongue flapping and my mind dizzy.

'Am I?' she said taking my hand and keeping it on her right thigh.

'You are' I said, limitlessly turned on. I ran my hand throw her arm slowly and later my hand was tracing her back. She didn't protest. She took my hand and placed it on her back. My body shook furiously. She came near me, her lips almost a centimetre away from mine.

'Don't you think we shouldn't be doing this?' I asked her, trembling. She didn't say anything. In the next moment, her lips were on mine.

Her mouth tasted the same as mine. The bitter-spicy-sweet taste was traced by my tongue. Her lips were soft. They felt like marshmallows. Sweet marshmallows.

We kept kissing unless I heard a glass break. She stepped aside, towards her side of the window. The sound was from outside.

I hastily got out of the car and froze. Dressed in blue T-shirt and jeans, a familiar shadow stood there. My heart stopped the moment I recognised the shadow. It was her. Mahira. She stood there, her face pale and expressionless. Diveesh stood right behind her. He looked confused.

'It's nothing like that…' I said. For the first time I had seen her cry. There was a glass box that lied shattered on the road that contained a blue coloured wrist watch.

She didn't move for a moment. She then stepped on the already broken glass and then started walking away.

'Mahira…' I said, holding her hand. She forcefully got free from my grip. She ran and ran.

'Mahira!' I tried to stop her. She ran and sat on her scooty. She started it without looking at me.

'Mahira!' I cried. She right through me, ignited her scooty and drove away as fast as she could.

'What the fuck!' I cried. I cried on the road. This couldn't happen. No, this couldn't. Please god. No. This can't happen. NOOOO!

'What happened?' Diveesh said, as he came running towards me.

'It was her…Mahira…' I said.

'Your ex?' he said and bit his tongue.

'How the fuck do you know this?' I spat.

'Where is my phone?' I shouted at him. With shivering hands, he took out my phone and starts to unlock it. I snatched it from him. His face was full of shock now.

I opened the messages and there was a message from her that was received this morning. It appeared as seen though I hadn't opened it. I read it.

I am sorry for breaking up with you. I am really sorry. We can surely do something to make this work out. I tried calling you but your number is appearing switched off. Meet me today, outside the Church, eight thirty. Please. I miss you. Even I have something to give to you. Do come.

I read the text again and again and clenched the phone in my hands. He knew it all. He…the motherfucker…knew it all…

Tear fell from my eyes as I read the words again. His face was expressionless now. I put the phone in my pocket.

'Why?' I said. He didn't respond. Kept looking down.

'I think I asked you something' I said. He still didn't reply.

A strong punch landed right on his nose that knocked him down. My hand was now covered with blood that flew from that cheap asshole's nose.

'WHY?' I shouted as I landed another punch in his chest.

'I…LOVED…HER' I said with strong punches landing after every pause. He coughed heavily.

'WHY DID YOU DO SO?' I slapped him. Grabbing his hair, I slammed his face in the street light's pole. There was a lot of blood.

'I ASKED WHY?' I said and kicked him.

'Because…I loved her…' he barely managed to speak.

'WHAT THE FUCK?'

'You took Mohini away from me, I took Mahira away from you' he said, 'Mohini still loves you. I love her so much, I wanted to tell her but before I could, you were already there. YOU TOOK HER AWAY FROM ME!' he spat blood on the road.

I raised my hand again but stopped.

'Promise me you'll never be angry' her words rang in my head.

I grabbed him from his T-shirt and rose him up.

'You are a blot on the name of friendship...a blot...you understand?' I shouted at him. He was still not in his senses.

I dragged him to his car and saw Mohini sleeping, snoring loudly.

'Drop...her...home...' I said, my brain finding it difficult controlling my hands.

'But...' he said.

'LEAVE BEFORE I KILL YOU!' I shouted. He hastily opened the driver's door and started to drive.

I sat next to the broken glass compartment that had the watch. The dial of the watch was now cracked and the needles were bended. I picked it up, a piece of glass cut right through my hand. I removed the glass and took out the watch. It looked beautiful. I hugged it tightly as blood flowed from different parts of my hand that were pierced with the broken glass. I took out my phone and called Mahira. The call automatically disconnected after one ring which meant that she had blocked me. I called Gourav.

'Can you come to take me?' I said, crying.

'Where are you? Why are you crying?' he asked.

'I'll answer every question of yours. First, just take me with you. I am here, outside the Church' I said.

'Five minutes' he said and hung up.

Epilogue

'Then?' He said. In the past one and a half hour, his face seemed like a roller coaster. He was smiling, frowning, angry, laughing, all at once. It was today, I had seen all the emotions possible for a human face to experience.

I started to cry, tears running through every part of my cheek possible. I wanted her, right now. I wanted to meet her. I wanted to tell her how much I love her. I wanted to hug her tightly and never let her go, ever.

'What happened then?' he asked, 'did you tell Gourav?'

'Yes, I did' I said. I didn't want to speak anymore. I took out the broken blue wrist watch out of my jean's pocket and clutched it tightly. She was so unfair with her decision. She could have listened to me but no, she decided to leave me midway. She was wrong.

'I told Gourav about it and then, in midnight, I sneaked out of the house to buy myself drinks and drank a lot, later sleeping and vomiting on my room's floor' I said, looking down, ashamed.

He looked up, as if thinking something.

'Oh…Sharief Sharief Sharief…' he said, 'that's really sad. Whatever that happened with you' he said.

'I am sick and tired of all this now. I don't want to live anymore. Damn, Google showed results of Suicide help lines' I said, sobbing.

'Ending your life won't make you some hero' he said, rolling his eyes.

'It's a great profession of yours. Hear to broken love stories and make money!' I snapped. He smiled.

'You didn't try to contact her again?'

'I didn't try? Every day. Every day, I waited outside her house, outside her school, outside the coaching centre. She looked right through me. My friends had informed her about my condition so she started texting me' I said.

'Texting you? What?'

'Just Good Morning and Good Night. Nothing else. It looks like an automated reply. Every morning at seven, there is her Good Morning and every evening at eight is her good night. Frankly, even her two texts are a painkiller for me!' I said.

'You should try to talk to her. You never tried to take up this topic?' he asked.

'My messages get no reply. I told you. She just texts me 'Good Morning' and 'Good Night'. Nothing else. I tried to take up this topic but there was never a reply from her.'

'You see, we can do nothing about this until you talk to her' he said, rubbing his eyes.

'Is there no solution to it? I am feeling so much depressed. I spend most of my time lost in a world of my own, crying, sulking. Please help me' I said, 'Please'.

'For now, I can give you nothing but Anti-Depressants. I hope they help you' he said.

'Anti-Depressants? Prozac?'

'Ah…Yes. The one they show in the books and all, a little less dosage though' he said and wrote furiously on his notepad.

He tore the page and handed it to me. It looked as if some ink had been spilled on the paper. Unfortunately, Doctors are like this only. Their handwriting puts aliens to shame.

'I am thinking of leaving Jammu' I said. He raised his eyebrow.

'Where are you going?' he asked.

'I am thinking of going to Gujarat. Will complete my studies there and try to get into a good medical college. I hope for the best. This town of ours is small. So small. I am sure to bump into her. The only way I think I will be able to forget her is going away from here' I said.

'It's all up to you. You can leave if you want to' he said. I looked at the wall clock. It was twelve.

I stood up to leave. The session felt useless and useful, both at the same time. Useless for I didn't get her back. Useful for I felt a little lighter now.

'If there's any way I can help you, please tell me' he said.

'Just don't tell anyone whatever I told you' I said.

'It can become a great novel' he said, 'only if you try to write it in a better way.'

'Novel? Seeing those five marks questions in the literature section make me shit in my pants every time and you want me to write a book? You in your senses doc?' I said and laughed.

'Only if you want to write it' he said. I shook my head.

'Great meeting you' I said and shook hands with him.

'I'll tell all my friends!' he said with childlike enthusiasm.

'What?'

'That I met MR Grey!' he said and I laughed.

'I am not Mr Grey. Grey was a winner. I am Mr Malhotra, the loser, the poor and ugly one' I said.

'Stop hating yourself!' he said.

'I will hate myself to infinity' I said.

'You'll never be able to love someone truly if you don't love yourself!' he said, probably recalling a line from some clichéd romantic movie.

'Some other day, Doc' I said.

'I am leaving for the States next week' he said, 'We'll keep in touch'

'Sure' I said and smiled. I got out of his home and called the driver.

In fifteen minutes, the driver arrived. I sat in the car and called my father.

'Hello…Dad…' I said.

'Yes. How was the session?' he asked, 'I hope you are over from your exam phobia.'

'Um…Dad…I want to leave the city' I said.

'Where will you go?'

'Gujarat, maybe. We have lived there for eight years. The quality of education is damn too high there! I want to go' I said, faking my tone to sound it excited enough. I had no interest in education now.

'We will think about it…' he said, 'I have a meeting. I have to go…Bye'

'Bye dad!' I said as the driver sped off.

HARD GOODBYES

'What are you doing?' my mother asked. I stared the screen of my laptop blankly with a new empty word file opened.

'Um...Trying to write something' I said.

'I hope your exams had gone well' she said, sipping water from the glass and passing me a disgusted look. I took my feet off the sofa.

'Yes, they have' I said with a smile. The past three weeks were heavily busy for me. I mugged through nights, crammed each and every concept and solved every question of our course. My exams had gone well and the result was going to be out soon. It was the first time I wasn't lying to them about my exams going well.

'Your dad talked to me...' she said.

'About?' I said, raising an eyebrow. Though I never bought those anti-depressants, I still didn't have much of food and sleep but felt relieved as I shifted all my focus towards my studies. I tried to call her for a last time. She picked and said nothing. There was no one on the other side. Fifteen minutes later, I hung up. If this was how it was meant to end, it should end like this.

'About you going to Gujarat...' she said, 'Why Gujarat only?'

'I am not specific. We were in Gujarat for eight years and you very well know what kind of atmosphere there is' I said.

Don't tell me that you have a Gujarati girlfriend. I don't want sweet Dals anymore in the house. Had enough of them for eight years' she said and laughed.

I started to write but failed. I closed the laptop and rested on the sofa.

Three hours later, my father was home. He wore a never seen before smile on his face.

'Why are you smiling dad?' I asked. He shook his head, still smiling.

'What?' I asked again.

'I have a surprise for you' he said and then smiled again.

'What surprise?'

He shook his head. Few more requests later, he took out a brown envelope from his bag.

'Here' he said, handing me the envelope.

'What is this dad?' I asked.

'Open it' he said. I carefully tore the envelope from the side and shook it. Two print outs fell from it. I picked both of them up and read. A smile ran on my face but my heart, it shrank.

One of the print out had a single flight ticket to Sardar Vallabhai International Airport the other was a two day stay in Hotel Hyatt Regency, Ahmedabad for next week.

'Be happy' he said as my face fell.

'Hey, what happened?' he said, putting his hand on my shoulder, you wanted to go, right?'

'Yes…' I barely managed to speak. I was acting like an asshole. It was my decision of leaving the city.

Though it meant I would be able to do some good with my life, it meant like a complete torture for me to survive without her.

Without seeing her, hearing her voice, making her smile. It was impossible to imagine.

'I have some work to do' I said as low as possible. I didn't want to cry in front of her.

'Okay' he said. Clutching the envelope in my hand I went in my room and bolted it from inside. Sitting on my knees on the floor, I cried.

It hurts when life suddenly takes a turn you never imagined and throws you off. This was it. I wanted to burn those tickets just like I had burn like the movies but deep inside, a voice inside me said that I may get myself a better life if I leave her...And the memories behind...

My phone rang. It was from an unknown number. I picked it up.

'Hello...' a female voice said. The voice was a bit heavy.

'Yes...' I said, controlling my tears.

'Sharief...' the person said from the other side.

'Mahira?' I said as she was the first one to hit my head.

'No...Mohini' she said, stuttering.

'What the fuck do you want now? Five years were not enough for you? ' I said.

'I am s...'

'Shut up! It's because of you I lost Mahira too. You kissed me, I didn't! You forced me to drink! You destroyed me.. ' I said, crying now.

There was a huge pause on the other side. I cursed heavily and cried.

'Sharief...' another female voice said. My ears alerted and the heart beat was fast. It was Mahira's voice.

'MAHIRA!' I cried.

'Sh...I am sorry Sharief...' she said.

'Don't be sor...' I said as she cut me mid sentence.

'I am an idiot. I am not perfect. I have flaws and I commit mistakes. Does this means you'll stop loving me?' she said and sobbed.

'I still love you' I said, 'I will till my last breath.'

'But what I did was wrong...' she said, 'I didn't gave you another chance. I was wrong...I am sorry...I love you too...I am sorry...' she said. I held my tears.

'How come are you with Mohini?' I asked.

'She came to my house today...She narrated me everything. Said that she was stressed and feared that she'll be in trouble so she acted like she was sleeping. She heard everything between you and Diveesh. She's a very nice girl!' she said.

I smiled. The intelligent feminist was nice. It was time that wasn't.

'But...' I said.

'But?'

'I am leaving...' I said, more of cried.

'Where are you going?' she asked.

'Gujarat...' I said.

'Wow. And when will you return? We'll go for a date! Not church this time though' she said and giggled.

'I am going forever. I won't come back. Will find some medical college there after 12th' I said.

'What?' she said.

'I am sorry...But I have to' I said, in an almost heartless tone.

'Why are you doing this to me?' she cried. It felt like a chainsaw ran right through my heart.

'I...am...sorry' I said.

'Please...don't do this to me' she said.

'I am sorry' I said as I heard a knock at my door. I hung up and opened the door. It was my dad.

'Its okay if you don't want to go' he said, 'we can refund the tickets.'

I wiped the tears off my cheeks.

'I will go' I said, 'I will'.

A Year Later

'We will miss you' Jyotsna, my neighbour since the past one year said.

'I will miss you guys too' I said.

Deactivating all my social networks, staying locked in the room for hours, mugging and being scarcely social for one year had finally brought some result. I had cleared the entrance exam with a descent rank and today, it was my flight to Delhi and my first day to college.

It's been a year since I've talked to Mahira or even texted her. Staring at her photos stored in my phone helped me. The past one year had been really interesting, with me writing a book. A broken love story. 'Breakup with a smile!'. It took me four months to write it and another five months to get through the publishing process.

Though not much of a bestseller, it's still quite famous among the youth. Well, it was weird to see an author with no social networking handle. Just his e-mail written below his photograph.

I had numerous e-mails. I renamed the characters to avoid from being sued for harassment. People found the book amazing. Some of them even mailed me that they cried after reading it. I was happy. I am happy.

I still love Mahira. You might be wondering that I am being heartless. Well, I am not. I want to meet her dressed in a white lab coat, with a stethoscope round my neck and a prefix of 'Dr.' Attached to my name.

'When will you meet her again?' she asked, raising her eyebrow.

'When time comes' I said.

'That's really UTSAV of you! When time comes!' she laughed.

'I hope you get your book published soon' I said.

'I don't have a broken love story dude. I have something special that only a few would get' she said.

'Yeah yeah. Whatever' I said, 'Okay. I have to go. Bye!' I hugged her tight. Being short, she stood on her toes to hug me. She was the only friend I had all this time.

The driver took the bag from me and put it in the trunk of the taxi. I opened the door and sat, looking at the pic of hers in which she was hiding her face with her hand. I had clicked it without telling her. A smile ran through my lips.

The airport was heavily filled. Gujju's love travelling by air. There was so much loudness and Gujarati in the environment. Ladies dressed in sarees roamed with heavy suitcases which probably contained Khakra and Fafda.

'Sir, would you please switch off your mobile phone?' the air hostess asked to the Gujarati businessmen sitting next to me.

'Tumhari yaad aavase' he said.

'Sir? Would you please switch it off?'

'Mara Putra su' he snapped, 'su thayu?' (It's my son! What happened?)

The air hostess shook her head and disappeared.

'Uncle phone *bandh kar lo*' I said. (Uncle, please switch it off)

'Arrey karu chu' he said and hung up, switching off his phone later.

Life was never easy without Radio cabs. I got one from the Indira Gandhi International Airport.

'Vardhaman Mahavir College' I said. He nodded.

It took half an hour to reach the college. The building read 'Vardhaman Mahavir College and Sarfdarjung Hospital, New Delhi'. I smiled, looking at it through the window. Hard work pays off.

'*Bas bas*' I said as the driver took out my only bag and started to walk into the main building.

I gave him three hundred rupees, fifty as a tip. Punjabi's love to give tips. Celebrations are incomplete without them.

I entered the college, like the hundreds others. I saw smiling faces, crying faces, ugly faces but not a single beautiful one. Well, you know whose one is the beautiful one.

Keeping my bag in the hostel room, I ran with a notebook, a pen and the biology text book in hand. The class started at one. It was one fifteen already.

I climbed the stairs as fast as I could and barged in through the door.

'Sir, may I come in!' I asked the professor through the half open door. He was a man with grey hair, dressed in pants buckled right below his Adams apple and had no interest in colour combinations.

'Yes. You are a late comer but still…The first day' he said and threw his hand in air.

I nodded and entered the class. It was full of some fifty students, mostly girls. They stared at me, one by one. I adjusted my specs to look a little nerd though my hairstyle didn't let me.

'So class…as I was telling' the professor said as he was interrupted by a female voice.

'Sir, may I come in?' a familiar hand, with pink nail polish applied carefully, appeared inside the room through the half open door.

'Ah…Another late comer' he grunted.

'Sorry sir' the voice said. My heart, mind and ears were now working in synchronization. It must be her. It must really be her.

The time became slow motion as I waited for the professors two magical words. Say it. Say it you god damn Einstein's surrogate son!

'Come in' the professor lipped as the door opened, and I felt a lightning from the sky striking my back. I stood up in a jerk, with my eyes wide, my mouth open, and my heart now beating just for the sake of formality. It was her. Miss Mahira Bhatt.

She startled when she saw me. Her eyes became big and then red. Her perfect lips were now muttering abuses to me, which sounded romantic no matter how much crass they were.

'Lets wait for another five minutes and see if there's any more late comer or not' the professor said. I didn't give a flying fuck for any other guy coming through the door now. The person I wanted, was now already sitting two desks away from me.

She kept looking at me, her eyebrows raised. She looked more beautiful than ever with Kohl applied on her eyes, dressed in a loose white T-shirt that had shades of blue and grey jeans. She was beautiful. I mean, she is beautiful.

The lecture ended two hours later. We kept looking at each other for the whole time. I didn't care what the rules of the institution were or how much great it meant to be a doctor from VMC.

As the bell rang, the professor left and everyone stood up to leave. Both of us, however were glued to our seats. Five more minutes later, the whole class was empty with only two of us sitting, the sound of the creaking fan and that of the pigeons.

'Hey!' I ran towards her but ran as the laces of my shoe trapped in the desk. She laughed but later frowned and made her *I am angry* face.

'Shit. Hey!' I said, sitting next to her.

She didn't reply. Didn't even look towards me.

'Hey' I said, placing my hand on her shoulder.

'Don't' she broke into tears, 'I said don't'

'Why?' I said. Tears fell on her notebook.

'You are a liar...You said you loved me' she said.

'I still do' I said.

'No you don't. If you did, you would have never left me' she said.

'I didn't leave you. Okay, I kind of did but I am sorry for it. I am sorry naa' I said.

'What do you think? Every time you'll do something stupid and then say Sorry? Is this enough? Do you know how hard I tried to find you? No, you don't. Do you know how much I missed you? Do you know how many copies did I buy of that book of yours? No, you don't. All you know is...' she said as I cut her mid sentence.

'I don't think those beautiful lips should be wasted for talking!' I said and bent towards her, closing my eyes. In another second, the world's most beautiful lips were on mine. I kissed her. She tasted of chocolate. Well, that's what she's been eating all this time. I kissed her again and again and she kissed back. She didn't protest. It was now that I could die in peace having kissed the world's most beautiful girl.

Exactly twenty three point five four nine seconds later, she leaned back. My eyes were still closed. A tight slap landed on my face.

'This for leaving me' she said.

'Ouch!! It hurts!' I shouted as her long fingers just hit my cheek.

'You…are…cute' she said pulling my cheeks hard.

'You…are…beautiful' I said.

'When two hearts really love each other, distance, age, time, money…all these are mere numbers for them!' I said.

'Aw…hey, I read this on Instagram last week!' she protested.

'It's been a year since I have left Instagram. It's an original. I mean surviving on sweet Dals, writing a book and clearing entrance exam. Have some respect for me!' I said. She grinned.

'Hey, I wrote some shayaries for you' I said as I took out the mini diary out of my jean's pocket.

She placed her head on her arms and listened to them, no matter how much boring, idiotic or shitty they were. A smile lit up her face every time I finished one. Her smile, the biggest achievement, even from writing a book or clearing entrance exams.

'How could one be so beautiful?' I asked, looking at her beautifully crafted face.

'Ask my parents' she said and giggled.